T0193211

Legends & Stories
for a Compassionate
America

Luigi Morelli

iUniverse LLC
Bloomington

OPEN BOOK
EDITIONS
A Berrett-Koehler Partner

LEGENDS AND STORIES FOR A COMPASSIONATE AMERICA

Book cover graphics: Megan Pugh
Editing: Colleen Shetland

iUniverse books may be ordered through booksellers or by contacting:

iUniverse
1663 Liberty Drive
Bloomington, IN 47403
www.iuniverse.com
1-800-Authors (1-800-288-4677)

ISBN: 978-1-4917-2745-4 (sc)
ISBN: 978-1-4917-2746-1 (e)

Printed in the United States of America.

iUniverse rev. date: 5/2/2014

Contents

Part II: Stories: Resisting the Nightmare

Introduction

I believe that we are lost here in America, but I believe we shall be found. And this belief, which mounts now to the catharsis of knowledge and conviction, is for me—and I think for all of us—not only our own hope, but America's everlasting, living dream.

—Thomas Wolfe

The thesis embraced in this book continues in time a previous research into the major turning points of Native North American history, seen through the eyes of the Maya, Aztecs, and Iroquois. The approach taken in that attempt is more imaginative since it seeks the correspondence between modern history and the myths and legends of Maya, Iroquois, and Aztecs. It is titled *Spiritual Turning Points of North American History,* and it takes a more specialized approach than the present volume.

A second theme intersects the first. What emerges from these pages is not turned to a nostalgic past, to a mere remembrance of old glories. As an early graduate of environmental sciences, I have been engaged in all aspects of right livelihood, from organic agriculture to socially responsible investments, alternative medicine, conscious consumerism, and communal living. In the American dream, themes of history and future intersect, chief of all being the yearning for a wholesale renewal of culture. It is clear that we are at the point of juncture of events and evolutionary possibilities that concern nation and globe.

From this intersection emerged the work I titled *A Revolution of Hope,* in which cultural renewal is approached as a key aspect of a paradigm shift that touches on all aspects of the human experience, including the spiritual. In that book, the examples of twelve step program, nonviolent communication, and social technology—so emblematic of the American soul—were explored for their deeper implications. The early concern for understanding the links between past and present, between historical foundations and an evolutionary future, is present in this further attempt.

The specific motivation for this work originated from my encounter with three works of art that crossed my path within a year, the same year in which I had moved from the West Coast to the East Coast. Each artistic expression (a movie, a legend, and a statue), not necessarily of great merit in and of itself, opened questions for which I simply wanted answers to put my curiosity to rest. The first set of questions to meet me was called up by the movie *Squanto: A Warrior's Tale*, a piece that did not impress me for its artistic achievements; the story, however, gripped me. The second questions came from a chance reading of a simplified version of the Iroquois legend of *The White Roots of Peace*, retracing the birth of the Haudenosaunee, or Iroquois League. Finally, the last question stands as a riddle in plain sight at Philadelphia's Penn's Landing in the form of the statue of Tamanend, so-called patron saint of the Pennsylvania colonists. With each encounter, I thought I would find answers simply by reading the appropriate book. But full answers were not forthcoming—or what I found did not exhaust my intellectual restlessness. On the contrary, the desire to know more was spurred each time, and I found myself becoming a researcher in the field of American legends, history, and biographies.

What precipitated this intense search lay in my biography. I was born in Washington, DC, but my father worked first for the World Bank, then for the United Nations, and then the European Common Market (now the European Union). So as a child I traveled the world, and then settled for most of my youth in Belgium. In my teenage years, an unspecified but persistent yearning always pulled at me from this side of the Atlantic. And finally, my return to the United States at age twenty-six (more specifically, landing in Santa Cruz, California) was the answer to that continuous pull.

Meeting America turned out to be completely different from any preconceived ideas I had harbored in my mind as a liberal-minded youth. With growing interest and a sense of discovery, I started to live the experience of being in this country, not only immersing myself in the new experiences that were offered to me, but also researching the history and mythos that informs much of what lives in the collective psyche of this country. Since everything was new for me, I could look at American history with freshness, unencumbered by the stereotypes and clichés that many Americans have met in their education, so much so that they have reached a saturation point. This freshness was a gift that allowed me to come to American history with curiosity and openness. Saturation reached me only much later, after I had had time to look at the commonly known and accepted history under a different lens.

Practically speaking, this book endeavors to combine both historical/scientific and artistic/intuitive perspectives. Legends, myths, and even biographies can be analyzed and dissected, and that is perfectly appropriate, but they can also be approached like holograms, like entities that can reveal their own gestures and intimate significance when we can live long enough with them without seeking to analyze their meaning. At some point, inspiration can come in, through which facts start speaking out of themselves and new images emerge. And that emergence should be perceived as a real discovery by the writer/ researcher.

Naturally I became interested in what the American dream has to offer or conceal. With time I came to accept an image that I had met: that this much-vaunted dream is like a precious antique painting that has been covered over with successive layers of paint of inferior quality. The new layers are all the interpretations, omissions, and deletions that have accumulated through two centuries of American history. At times the dream recedes so far from the national consciousness that it may much more resemble a nightmare—as it does at present in many ways. And the initial dream may be exploited for opportunistic reasons, to influence us in one direction or the other. Truth be told, the dream is barely alive for most of American society. So how can we recapture it? In this effort, I want to give voice to something deeper than interpretations: to the power that is present in images, legends, the threads of remarkable biographies, and the work of remarkable pioneers who could lead us into a new and enlivened future.

This book has had two phases, two geneses. In its first edition, it was called *Hidden America: The Spiritual Legacy of the Nation's Founding Fathers and the Nation's Native Ancestors*. In its original form, the book contained only three sections, which focused on the past of the nation's history (the first three chapters of part I). As I set out to revise, three chapters were added, and what was begun as a look into the past expanded into the present. These three additional chapters follow American history up to the twentieth century (part II).

Even though this book moves from the past into the present, it is not conceived, nor meant to be read, as a chronological sequence; rather, it is intended as a series of tableaux or vignettes. Each chapter is conceived as an aspect of the American dream: America as the land of the free, America as the land where "all men are created equal," and America as the land of opportunity. These could be called the yearning for freedom, for equality under a fuller democracy, and for economic justice. These themes come in recurring forms over the centuries, no matter how alive or spent the dream may be in its manifest form.

Three themes come from the past origins of the nation or earlier (part I); the same three themes are followed up, continued, and renewed in three other stories (part II), emblematic of the whole development that has led us into the twentieth century.

This book has gone through a long gestation since I first started it more than ten years ago. I repropose it now, after many changes and much re-elaboration, sensing that its message is timely, that it is not too late for a compassionate America to truly find itself anew. And I offer it because images and stories speak louder than elaborate interpretations. None of the images offered could possibly be exhausted by what particular coloration may be given here. Therefore it is my hope that they will continue to live in you, the readers, and inspire you in the pursuit of a kinder future for the United States of America.

Part I:

Legends and Stories: Giving Shape to the American Dream

Fellow citizens, the signers of the Declaration of Independence were brave men. They were great men too— great enough to give fame to a great age. It does not often happen to a nation to raise, at one time, such a number of truly great men.

—Frederick Douglass

Chapter 1

From Tamanend and Washington:
The Dream of Freedom

The usual hero adventure begins with someone from whom something
has been taken, or who feels there is something lacking in the normal
experience available or permitted to the members of society. The
person then takes off on a series of adventures beyond the ordinary,
either to recover what has been lost or to discover some life-giving
elixir. It's usually a cycle, a coming and a returning.

—Joseph Campbell

*a*t the eastern end of Market Street in Philadelphia, overlooking
the Delaware River at Penn's Landing, is a ten- or twelve-foot bronze
statue, green with time, of a Native American with long flowing hair.
Standing on his shoulder is an eagle that holds the famous wampum
belt of the Great Peace Treaty signed by William Penn with the Lenni-
Lenape in 1682. An inscription indicates that this is Tamanend, the
American patron saint held in great esteem by the colonists, whose feast
is celebrated yearly on May 1.

One sunny day while walking around Penn's Landing, I came
across this statue. Although I had lived in the Philadelphia area for
more than a year, I had never heard of Tamanend, but seeing the statue
stirred something in me that was hard to define. Here was a Native
American held in high esteem, celebrated as a patron saint. I wanted
to know more and decided to inquire first of all in the libraries and
bookstores. The most common response was, "Who?" I would repeat,
just as incredulously, that there was a large statue in a prominent spot
in the city that represented Tamanend, but at first my search yielded
nothing. I expanded my search from the public libraries into college

1

libraries. This was before the days of the Internet, so my interest directed me toward old manuscripts and microfilms. What little I found spurred my interest and imagination further.

The figure of Tamanend was linked over time to that of George Washington. A cultural leader of the past was associated with a cultural leader of the time, even if the latter was primarily a man of action. The American Revolution gathered truly exceptional individuals at a unique time in history. Benjamin Franklin towered above them all, and was an even greater American cultural figure than Washington. We will return to him at the end of this chapter, and we will revisit both Washington and Franklin in the next.

Tamanend: The Birth of a Legend

There is little historical record to substantiate much more than Tamanend's physical existence. He is most likely a conglomerate of historical figure, legend, and popular folklore. The following will offer a taste.

On a microfilm in a university library, I found a myth created and recorded in 1795 by an early American scholar, Samuel Latham Mitchill.[1)] In this narrative, Tamanend (called Tammany in this source) faced seven tests, overcoming seven states of evil, and thereby became a spiritual initiate and civilizing hero. The first three ordeals involved natural catastrophes, which Tamanend overcame through the use of natural remedies. Mitchill's version follows:

> The evil spirit, Makimanito, first spread poison sumac and stinging nettle all over the land in such density that it choked all other plants; the poisoning of the air also affected all the tribes. But Tamanend caused a drought, and consequently was able to extinguish the poisonous plants through fire. In the suddenness of Tamanend's attack, the evil spirit was caught unguarded and remained singed by the fire. For the second test, the evil spirit turned to the animal kingdom, and brought from the north herds of mammoths and other carnivorous animals that nourished themselves on human flesh. None of the weapons

the natives used could cause the animals any significant wound. Tamanend knew that these monsters liked salt, and he asked the tribes to procure vast quantities of it. They spread it over large areas, and in that way they could easily corner the animals and trap them. The evil spirit then turned to the help of the elements, particularly water. It fell in abundance and flooded the whole territory. The waters rose high above the normal level in the lakes Erie, Huron, and Michigan. From there the waters would have poured in abundance toward the south. But Tamanend received word of what was happening, and opened dams through which the waters would flow into the Allegheny, Miami, and Wabash Rivers; he also cut a ditch that turned into the present Ohio River. The remaining Niagara Falls are a witness to this mighty attack of the evil one and Tamanend's wisdom.

The fourth attack came in the form of war declared by neighboring tribes. Tamanend vanquished the attackers, and then showed them clemency; he reconciled them with unexpected generosity and brought about a lasting peace.

In the turning point of the myth, the evil one, Makimanito, decided to treacherously attack Tamanend, attempting to drown him in the waters of the Ohio River. After a fifty-day battle, Tamanend subjugated the foe, but without totally vanquishing him. Makimanito was banished to the cold regions of the far north.

Tamanend dedicated himself to the arts of peace: the introduction of new agricultural practices, such as growing corn and beans, making bread from corn, and using tobacco infusions to repel flies and mosquitoes. To these was added the apple that evolved from the native crab-tree. Nor was Tamanend idle in the technological field; he introduced the use of birch bark and resin that allowed the building of waterproof canoes. Likewise he offered improvements in the making of bows and arrows.

After some years, chief Tamanend's reputation spread far and wide. He was called upon to journey to offer his wisdom to the young Inca nation. Reluctantly, the tribes accepted that they must let go of their spiritual leader He made sure that every safeguard would be in place for the preservation of his people in his absence. While he was away, Makimanito attacked the tribes' moral fiber. Idleness and depravity gave rise to illness and disease. Returning, Tamanend healed the people through his knowledge of the properties of medicinal herbs, such as dogwood bark and sarsaparilla. And this is how he became an initiate of the Medewiwin, a civilizing hero.

Before the advent of the Iroquois League in the 1400 to 1500s, the Lenape had formed a league. Tamanend's reign occurred at a time when the Lenni-Lenape had lost their splendor and had been subjugated by the Iroquois. His name rarely appears in any official document, although presumably he was the sachem, leader of the Lenni-Lenape, the people who brought about the Great Peace Treaty with William Penn. But no historical documents give proof of it. The peace resulting from the treaty lasted beyond Penn's death for at least thirty-six years, when it was broken by the colonists.

Native American culture was difficult for the colonists to accept and integrate, and for the most part it was stamped out. Nevertheless, it continued to exert attraction and fascination for many, even if in a romanticized fashion. A useful parallel or analogy that can serve to some extent as a comparison is the relationship the Romans had with conquered Greece. Greece was occupied by the Romans, who had a superior military organization. Nevertheless, Greek culture later permeated much of Roman civilization; witness the Roman assimilation of the Greek pantheon of gods. Native American civilization was wiped out by the colonists; still, the impulses that lived in their culture were not completely blotted out and even exerted a strong influence for the good. This will become all the more apparent when we examine Iroquois culture in chapter 2.

As I did more research, I found that the name "Tamanend" literally means "beaver-like." It can also be translated as "affable," because the beaver was considered the most sociable of animals by the Lenape. The legendary affable Native American leader was transformed by the colonists into a patron saint. His career as a saint followed a circuitous path. The first mention appeared in 1732 in the records of the Schuylkill Fishing Company. At that time, it was a common custom for groups to adopt a patron saint, and the company had taken Tamanend as their own. The fishing season began on May 1; hence that day was adopted as a day to celebrate their saint Tamanend.

From King to Saint: From Tamanend to Washington

Tamanend's career blossomed, and he became ever more popular with the colonists. He was frequently invoked as a reason for riotous celebrations, especially on May Day, and various societies claimed him as their saint.

At some point, the friendly saint was reborn as a patriotic character. This was probably around the year 1765, when colonial resistance to the British crown surged after the passing of the Stamp Act. In the press, Tamanend's name was anglicized to King Tammany, in obvious contradistinction to King George III.

A word should be given here about the most famous (or infamous) of the Societies of St. Tammany, New York City's Tammany Hall, also known as the Columbian Order, founded in 1786. By the end of the nineteenth century, this society had become a political organization used by the Democratic Party, and over time it played a major role in controlling New York City and New York State politics. It is most often remembered as a channel for political patronage and graft. This association of the name Tammany with corruption occurred, however, long after the birth of the Tammany myth.

Mixing Traditions

Originally the holiday celebration blended the Celtic tradition of the maypole with Native American overtones. A description of a 1771 May Day celebration at Annapolis indicates that a maypole, decorated with flowers and ribbons, was erected in the middle of the square or other public location. The dancers, each holding a ribbon, moved in a circle around the pole. A small band played pennywhistles, drums, and other instruments. Yet, upon closer examination, one could notice something odd. The participants were performing dances in a Native American style. In the midst of the performance, the company was interrupted by the arrival of people dressed as Native Americans, whooping and singing the war song. After completing their appearance, the newcomers collected money and retired satisfied. It was the custom for the participants on this day to wear a piece of bucktail, symbol of liberty, on a hat or any other prominent part of their dress.[2]

The festivities were followed with the recitation of songs and poems, in which Tammany was remembered and exalted, often with a mix of solemnity and humor. One can also witness the humor in these lines from a Pennsylvania celebration in 1786:

> We, Pennsylvanians these old tales reject,
> And our own saint think proper to elect;
> Immortal Tammany, of Indian Race!
> Great in the Field, and foremost in the chace![3] (*Character of St.*
> *Tammany*, popular poem written by William Pritchard in 1786)

The obvious Celtic connection to the holiday described above is that the Celts celebrated Beltane on May 1, one of their four cardinal yearly celebrations and one of their major sacred days. The May Day celebrations have survived to this day in the tradition of the maypole dance. From these two traditions, early America created a pagan saint—a syncretistic celebration of Celtic and Native American inspiration.

In 1772, the first permanent society in Philadelphia to be named after Tammany was named the Sons of King Tammany, a name echoing the Sons of Liberty, of Boston Tea Party fame. Later in that year, the press started referring to the native leader as either king or saint.

At the beginning of the Revolutionary War, the Pennsylvania troops adopted Tammany as patron and guide. Shortly after that, the Continental Army followed suit. By that time, May Day was observed both at home and on the field, and had clearly taken on a larger dimension than the borders of Pennsylvania. It was in the same year, 1776, that John Leacock wrote a successful patriotic play titled: "The Fall of the British Tyranny, or American Liberty Triumphant." An ode in this satire, written in honor of Saint Tammany in a rather humorous tone, became popular and was later sung at the celebrations of the numerous Tammany Societies that sprang up. Tammany's image even found its way into the national flag on May 1, 1785, in Philadelphia.[4]

Tamanend Becomes a Symbol

The symbolic status of Tamanend was never an intentional design. It seems rather to have followed a natural progression from jest to eventual defiance. The saint's popularity did not abate after independence was achieved. Stories and songs flourished from 1773 to 1789. Samuel Latham Mitchill's myth, mentioned earlier, was recorded in 1795.[5]

The saint's reputation spread as far south as Louisiana and as far north as New York. Farther north, the saint would have made odd company with Puritan traditions because the Pilgrims disapproved of wild celebrations. This attitude dated since at least 1620, when the Pilgrims were in an uproar over the May Day revels at Merry Mount (near Plymouth Rock). Still, it is very likely that the Boston Sons of Liberty were in contact with the various Tammany Societies, and such a link has been established for the Saint Tamina [sic] Society of Annapolis, Maryland. That the Sons of Liberty also adopted some of the Native American values and disguises is widely known. The famous Boston Tea Party of 1773 was performed by forty or fifty patriots dressed as Mohawks. Finally, although the New Englanders didn't dance around the maypole, they assembled more soberly around the Liberty Tree.

The Saint Tammany societies were later revived in the Orders of Red Men and the Improved Orders of Red Men, which claim to be the oldest fraternal organizations to be chartered in this country.[6] The Orders of Red Men preserved the observance of Saint Tammany's Day, but moved it to May Day to May 12. Their motto was "freedom, friendship, and charity," and their ritual had all the ethos of Freemasonry.

Tamanend and Washington

The reviving of the Tammany ideal in conjunction with Masonry and the canonization of Tammany the king point back to a time when the process of initiation was still possible and was practiced within the sacred centers. Tamanend was both a spiritual and a political leader; we may say he was a political leader precisely because first and foremost, he was a spiritual leader. It was in his status as an initiate that he could infuse spiritual values into his culture, and therefore bring the blessings of peace. The choice of May Day, which was said to be a day of openness between the physical world and the spiritual world, reinforces this meaning.

At the time of the colonies, the medieval concept of the enlightened king was coming to an end, not only in Europe, but also in North America. This tradition had already been supplanted by the Iroquois democratic impulse, as we will see in the next chapter. In the earlier times of the colonies, especially on the East Coast, many Native American confederacies still existed, ruled by the equivalent of a king. We will examine two of them in chapter 3: the Powhatan confederacy in Virginia and the Wampanoag confederacy in Massachusetts. Tamanend stood both as a beginning and an end: a beginning in that he inspired ideals for the American Revolution, and an end inasmuch as the monarchy gradually gave way to new, more complex forms of government.

The Tammany Societies throughout the colonies named Washington as their grand sachem. Before becoming the country's first president, Washington had accumulated many other honorific titles. He was the president of the Cincinnatus Society, an organization founded by army officers and committed to a strong union. The Pennsylvania Grand Lodge, in 1779, had harbored the idea of a nationwide Grand Lodge, with Washington as its president, and Virginia chose him as the Grand Lodge Master in 1778, but he declined both positions.

Washington's birthday was honored with festivities for the first time in 1782, on the occasion of his fiftieth birthday, in Richmond, Virginia. It was celebrated the following year with a banquet in New York, and repeated in 1784 after the withdrawal of the English troops. Until that time, Washington's birthday had not been a recurring celebration. That came about with the inauguration of Washington's first term as president. This celebration came in great part through the initiative of the Tammany Societies, especially in New York. For that reason, some did in fact call it the Tammany Observance. Washington's name was associated in jest with his illustrious predecessor, as it appears from the lines of the "Ode for Saint Tammany's Day":

Now each Sachem join hands round the Liberty Pole,
And briskly again pass the heart cheering bowl;
To Washington's mem'ry, the chief of our train,
The full flowing goblet repeated we'll drain....
                    from "Ode for St. Tammany's Day," May 1, 1785 [7)]

Although a piece of doggerel and certainly written in jest, these lines show a deeper understanding of the figure of Washington, elevating him to the status of the "affable saint" and civilizing hero. That the patron saint would receive a human counterpart was not any great departure from tradition. The British crown and other monarchies honored both king and saint; there was a feast day for Saint George, as much as the king had his own. This tradition hearkened back to the king as the agent of divine will on earth. However, in 1782, the very first year in which his birthday was celebrated, Washington refused the crown offered to him by a Colonel Lewis Nicola in the name of the Continental Army. Perhaps Washington realized that an era had come to an end. We can appreciate what stood behind the figure of Washington by observing the most characteristic, but sometimes overlooked or underestimated, elements of his life.

Recurring Themes in George Washington's Life

This brief biography of Washington will also serve as an introduction to the following chapter. Washington's life marked a transition, and we will show how he brought a certain ideal to a culmination and end—precisely what can be called the Tammany ideal. On the other hand, Washington inaugurated a new epoch, as we will see in the following chapter.

Background to Colonialism in North America

Understanding a national figure requires some basic understanding of national and international phenomena. Central to coming to terms with the individuality of George Washington is a basic knowledge of what some have called mercantilism, the unstated economic doctrine of British imperialism. Therefore, in order to better understand

Washington and the times in which he lived, we turn to the economic arena of life at the time of the colonies.

The factors that led to the American Revolution are often attributed to the Stamp Act, the Townsend Acts, and the Navigation Acts, suggesting that these marked a sudden change in the nature of the relationship between mother country and colonies. These acts, however, were in fact merely final steps, the catalysts of the rebellion; they were simply the logical outcome of the kind of economic relationships that had ruled ever since the beginning of the colonies.

After the Middle Ages, the economic growth of nations would have been inconceivable without the growth of military power to sustain it. Wealth was conceived of in terms of gold and silver, and economic advantage derived from a favorable balance of trade. England expected exactly that from America, as from any other colony. Thus, as early as 1660, economic activity and growth were everywhere regulated or curtailed on American soil by the Council of Trade (later called the Board of Trade). No export could leave America for a third country without first going to England. Imports to the colonies of non-English origin were subject to duties. In practice, trade was in the hands of what could be called true monopolies, and middlemen realized large profits at the expense of the colonists. It has been estimated that the balance of trade between the colonies and England, resulting from the combined effects of the English policies between the years 1700 and 1773, was 30 million pounds in favor of England. Part of that amount served to pay the internal debt of the crown. This debt amounted to 74 million pounds in 1775; the interest on this sum was 2.4 million. After the Seven Years' War, the principal increased by 72 million and the interest by nearly 2.5 million.[8]

Among the consequences resulting from the rules made by the Board of Trade were the repeated prohibition of manufacturing activities, prohibition of exports, and finally, the curtailing of the growth of the territories because of the difficulty of enforcing the law over an ever-growing expanse of land.[9] The reaction to rampant smuggling was searches without warrant and trials without jury. These actions crippled the northern colonies; the southern colonies experienced a de facto economic enslavement.

The situation of the South is eloquently summarized in the words of Murray N. Rothbard:

> In the South, British mercantilism found its ultimate logical outcome in the system of plantations operated by slaves. Ever since the introduction of tobacco, codified monopolistic practices had been enforced. In 1619, the Crown was already imposing duties on colonial tobacco. Two years later it prohibited colonists from selling tobacco to any other country without first landing in England and paying the duty. The following year, the Virginia Company was awarded monopoly on imports in England and Ireland. When the planters started to sell tobacco to other colonies, especially New England, a prohibitive duty eliminated that possibility. The net result of these policies was to drastically reduce the price of tobacco, while the price of imported goods was beyond the colonists' control. This chain of events ushered in the extensive use of slaves, and hence the slave trade, over which the British had acquired the monopoly following wars with the Dutch. Before the Navigation Acts, the southern colonies could sell their tobacco to the Dutch for three pence per pound. By 1767, after the Navigation Acts, tobacco prices had fallen to a half penny per pound. The same Navigation Acts raised the prices of imports, which were now confined to British ships. More competitive sources, notably the Dutch, had been precluded. English laws prevented the South from restricting the slave trade. For equivalent reasons New England and the Middle Colonies later became major actors in the slave trade.[10]

Mercantilism can be defined as the complete identification of economic and political interests. Where economic competition was barred from exerting its benefits, mercantilism could be supported only with the complicity of the political system. A prominent political class, and often the crown itself, benefited in England from the formation of immense economic monopolies. Although on the one hand, English tradition advocated the liberties of the Englishman; on the other hand, economic monopolies were promoted at the expense of these very same liberties. America was unique among the colonies of European powers in that here mercantilism was imposed, not upon a native population, but for the most part upon subjects of His Majesty, who were well acquainted with the tradition of individual liberties. It is significant that from the indebted and economically shackled South came George Washington, a Virginia native.

Washington's Constitution and Temperament

Washington had unusually striking and prominent physical features and an imposing stature. He had very large hands, joints, and feet, and long arms and legs. His hips were broad, and his neck has been described as "superb" by George Mercer. Washington also had a large mouth. He was literally head and shoulders above the rest.

As might be imagined, Washington possessed a robust physical constitution. As a youth he had a taste for activities that demanded physical prowess. He was an excellent horse rider and renowned dancer. His life was filled with brushes with death or illness. He survived malaria at seventeen, smallpox two years later, and dysentery at age twenty-five. In 1789 he had a tumor removed from his thigh, and the following year came close to dying from a combination of influenza and pneumonia. Another example illustrates his physical strength. At age twenty-one, Washington was attempting to cross the partly frozen Allegheny River in a raft. The raft became stuck in the ice, and Washington fell overboard. He had to spend a chilling night on an island until he could cross over the frozen river the next day. Amazingly, he survived without consequences. In contrast, his companion Christopher Gist's fingers were all frozen, and some toes as well.

At age twenty-one Washington joined the Fredericksburg, Virginia, Masonic Lodge. Masonry provided a continuing thread in Washington's life, and much of his outlook can be understood in light of it. For him, Masonry was not an abstract philosophy, for which he had little inclination; it was a code of honor that could pervade and accompany all his actions. Masonic loyalties molded the relationships within the army, and a Masonic inauguration brought him to the presidency. Of this more will be said later. Washington also had a regular and deep life of prayer. He ordered prayers to be said in the army every morning and on Sunday. When no chaplain was available, he would say the prayers himself. We can detect in him deep spiritual leanings.

Washington also had ambition, pride, and an impulsive nature; however, he displayed quite other qualities as well. He was a reticent and careful speaker and a good listener. He was also sensitive to what others thought of him. Washington was thin-skinned and would remain so practically to the end. Forgoing popular support was a major test that he encountered repeatedly.

Washington had abundance of will, and his need to release the overabundance in order to devote it for a higher purpose found a fitting symbol in the odd way in which he cared for his teeth. It is hard to imagine what would induce a man to lose practically all his teeth from cracking walnuts between his jaws and to endure the pain of the ensuing inflammations and the irritation of a denture carved from hippopotamus tusks. This exuberance of will was also displayed in his early military exploits.

The First Forty-Two Years

Turning points in Washington's biography coincide with major events in American history. At age twenty-one he volunteered to go on a diplomatic mission to France shortly before the French and Indian War. Soon after, he started his military career in that conflict. Exactly twenty-one years later, this constellation of events reoccurred on a higher level. It was again a turning point between diplomatic efforts and a call for action, this time between the British and the colonials. He was chosen as a Virginia delegate to the First Continental Congress, and a year later he was named commander in chief of the Continental Army.

The first forty-two years of Washington's life formed a stage of apprenticeship. During this period, the obstacles put in his way by the reality of the colonial situation and of his times gave him many opportunities to temper his ambition and impulsiveness. In more ways than one, Washington was a quintessential representative of the grievances of his compatriots. As a planter, he was deeply indebted and had to devise continuous attempts toward self-sufficiency and independence because the system of monoculture made the plantation system a captive market of the English monopolies. His military career met with setbacks as well as success. First joining the British Continental Army, he was promoted to colonel at Fort Necessity, only to be demoted to the rank of captain later, an offer that he turned down. After performing heroically as an aide-de-camp for the British Colonel Braddock, Washington was named commander in chief of the British Continental Army, but he had to take second place to Dagworthy, a captain, since the latter had been appointed by Royal Commission and Washington was only a colonial. On the political front, Washington keenly felt how little power was vested in the Virginia House of Burgesses, which was dissolved twice during his tenure when it tried to promote colonial economic independence.

Washington reached the conclusion that a break with Britain was inevitable. His conclusion was not based on the grounds of the ideals of Jefferson or Madison, but on his inner knowledge deriving from experience, which led him to take what he perceived as the right action. It was the realization of the South's economic dependence that led him to embrace the colonies' nonimportation agreements in response to the Stamp Act. He went further on a personal level by turning away from growing tobacco, and developing small processing industries on his lands instead. By this time, he had paid off his debt to Cary and Company, his British suppliers.

Tempering the Will

From the experience of the first forty-two years, Washington had gained knowledge of how to temper his will. This quality enabled him to take on the task of leading the new Colonial Continental Army. During the Revolutionary War, he had to constantly relinquish personal power in favor of the possibility of a new social experiment. Later on, after the victory of the Revolutionary War, Washington vigorously exerted his power to defend the precarious new government against the dangers that threatened it from the outside—in particular, the political threat of the French Revolution and the economic threat of the British.

During the war, Washington had to coordinate his activities with the Continental Congress. He fully understood the importance of a transparent, if not harmonious, cooperation with that political body. Soldiers, politicians, and civilians had to be won over to the ideals of the Declaration of Independence, not once, but over and over again. Thus, Washington endured all delays, divisions, and hesitations on the part of Congress. Likewise he did not retaliate personally against insubordination or political scheming within the army. However, when the need called, he stood up against the Conway Cabal, an alliance of high officers and members of Congress who plotted to remove Washington from the high command. In 1782 the army, through a Colonel Lewis Nicola, offered to crown Washington as king. Absolute power was within reach, and Washington refused it. The following year, he used all his personal influence to quell army mutinies and insurgency against Congress.

That the Constitutional Convention owes much to Washington's presence as chairman is beyond doubt. His was a silent presence, although it was no less powerful for that fact. His stature and integrity contributed in large measure to the success of the convention.

The New Republic, Balanced Between England and France

Washington had the capacity to hold a middle ground between polarizing extremes. Two significant sets of events stand out in Washington's presidency, which illustrate those extremes and his holding the middle. First was the test posed by the French Revolution; the second was the continuing English imperialism. Agents of the French Revolution were actively proselytizing around the world. In America, the French Revolution's envoy was *Citoyen* Genet. Washington had initially reacted favorably to the French political change. With time, the flaring of passions, the report of atrocities, and the death toll from the guillotine made a different impression on President Washington. In 1793, war broke out between France and England, and Washington opted for a course of strict neutrality. That was Washington's first trial of standing against popular opinion, and he prevented the young country from being engulfed in the violence of French revolutionary zeal.

On the English front, Washington concluded the Jay Treaty with

England in 1795, which was also very unpopular. Although many disapproved of the favorable concessions given to England, the treaty was probably the most the United States could hope for, considering its obvious state of economic and military inferiority. At any rate, the treaty allowed the nation to turn away from the European turmoil and build its own strength while avoiding war.

America's situation on the international front, standing in the middle between the extremes manifested by France and England, found a reflection within the Washington administration. Thomas Jefferson, Secretary of State, and Alexander Hamilton, Secretary of the Treasury, were in every respect polar opposites. The young Thomas Jefferson was a man of passionate ideas, at moments naïve perhaps, but always sincere. Hamilton had high intellectual capacities. He was a stern realist and a very ambitious one. His love for the new country was for the most part a love of its government. The difference between the two men is reflected in the nature of the departments the two antagonists headed.

Hamilton was a strong supporter of England, and he would have modeled the new nation in many respects according to the old one.[11] He was also in favor of a strong centralism and often opted for displays of force before negotiation. However, he was probably one of the few who had the capacity to lead the nation to financial independence. In contrast, Jefferson was a very strong supporter of states' rights and had been won over in a very determined way to the ideas of the French Revolution.[12] He later regretted his youthful ardor.

France's policy was a sort of all-or-nothing attempt to try to win sympathy and support from the United States. The ideas of the French Revolution could truly enflame people's minds in a rapturous passion, much as they did Jefferson's. England, on the other hand, could gain support for its plans by cultivating the appropriate politician in the right place, much as it tried to do through Hamilton. English strategies for change were disguised in the tools of trade and finance. Through these tools the English could modify the direction of the American nation more effectively than through any other political means.

Washington held the ground between the extremes of oligarchy (represented by Hamilton) and pure democracy (represented by the young Jefferson). America became a republican government, as distinguished from a pure and simple popular democracy. The president knew how to use the two men's strength for the goals that the nation needed to achieve: foreign recognition and economic independence.

American Cultural Heroes: Washington and Franklin

The Tamanend tradition humorously equated Washington with the Indian patron saint; that was, undoubtedly, an ironic detour of popular wisdom. What about this intuition? In the figure of Tamanend reecho traits of the great spiritual teacher known by the name Deganawidah, who lived and taught in the American Northeast, not far from Tamanend's Philadelphia. The tradition of this great initiate of the Americas, Deganawidah, overshadows Tamanend himself.

We can call the composite figure of Tamanend a cultural or civilizing hero, someone who can give a new evolutionary impulse to his people. Among Tamanend's feats are the introduction of agricultural practices and technological innovations that allowed new growth of population, and the blessings of a general state of peace among the tribes. But those innovations are just the consequences of a general reassessment of values, through which the whole of society operated at a new evolutionary stage. Everyone was elevated, and all of society benefited. Tamanend could achieve this only because of the inspiration that he received from the Great Spirit. Tamanend could be considered this continent's equivalent of a Buddha. Although it is less obvious to us, America too has had its great teachers, those through whom new cultural steps could be achieved. Tamanend is a composite created in the collective mind, representing the role of a great teacher and leader. Nevertheless, the composite points to a real historical figure, as Latham Mitchill intuited in the myth he delivered in his oration, which was referred to earlier.

What do we find in Washington that makes him unique? We have described an individual who was exceptional even from the physical standpoint—for instance, his stature, his physical prowess, his seemingly indifferent attitude in his brushes with death. But that is only a beginning. Washington had a lifelong cultivation of character that describes a unique trajectory. An incredible force of will led him from an early, undifferentiated ambition to a complete dedication to an ideal that he served unswervingly. His deep inner life, which can be perceived in his life of prayer and his devotion to the ideals of Freemasonry, allowed him to mold and curb his own willful temperament and offer it in service to the whole. At no time did he exercise his tremendous willpower against Congress or his opponents. He espoused a complete alignment of means and ends. And this resolve culminated in his selfless renunciation of power, one of those rare historical gestures that set a precedent. He first renounced a crown, and later renounced power after his second term as president. No ruler before him in history had ever willingly done so.

This seemingly small gesture by Washington—renouncing power—paved the way for something the world had not known before: government of the people, by the people. With Washington, the new world stepped into the next stage of reality. It is hard to measure how much of this was due to the figure of one man. It is clear that he worked in conjunction with many others, but, together with Benjamin Franklin, he took a leading role. Washington truly was the equivalent of a Tamanend, a first one, a moral and spiritual leader to the nation. It is no doubt for this reason that in the time of deepest despair, in the winter of Valley Forge, a vision was vouchsafed to Washington that confirmed what has been said so far about him and presented the dimension of his deeds in the unfolding history of the United States.

Washington's Vision for the Future of the United States

At Valley Forge, Washington was surprised and pleased at the loyalty of his men, but still very much at a loss to see a clear path. At this point in his life, Washington turned, more than ever, to his life of prayer, believing that the American people were guided and protected by the agency of divine providence. He felt that he himself had been protected from bullets and illnesses in innumerable circumstances.

In the winter of 1778, when all seemed hopeless, Washington, deeply alone and discouraged, had been praying and meditating in the woods. His aide, Anthony Sherman, had been building a fire for Washington, who was working at a dispatch. Washington's words were recorded by Sherman: "This afternoon, as I was sitting at this table engaged in preparing a dispatch, something seemed to disturb me. Looking up [in front of the fire] I beheld standing opposite a singularly beautiful female."[13] And further: "My thought itself became paralyzed! A new influence, mysterious, potent, irresistible, took possession of me! All I could do was gaze steadily, vacantly at my unknown visitant." Finally, the general found his voice to inquire about the presence. He did so four times without receiving an answer.

The presence took on a new form. "Gradually the surrounding atmosphere seemed filled with sensations, and grew luminous. Everything about me seemed to rarefy; the mysterious visitor herself becoming more airy and yet more distinct to my sight than ever." What is most interesting about this stage was the change in Washington's consciousness. "I next began to feel as one dying, or rather to experience the sensation which I sometimes imagined accompanies dissolution [death]. I did not think, I did not reason. I did not move. All that was impossible. I was conscious only of gazing fixedly at my companion."

Washington's change of consciousness made possible the revelations of the being, who called for Washington's attention: "Son of the Republic, look and learn!" The being then took Washington to a spiritual landscape in which he saw, as if spread out in front of him, the continents of the earth. The angelic vision, "dipping water out of the ocean in the hollow of each hand," sprinkled some of the water over America and some over Europe. A cloud arose from each side of the ocean, converging over the waters, then moving to the west and enveloping America. The process was repeated a second time, and a third. After the third time, Washington saw villages, towns, and cities filling the landscape, one after another.

What happened next can only have seemed shrouded in mystery to the general, so prophetic were its images of times yet to come. Later published in the *National Tribune* (Dec. 1880), it is worth quoting at length.

And with this the dark, shadowy figure turned its face southward, and from Africa I saw an ill-omened specter approaching our land. It flitted slowly over every city and every town of the latter.

The inhabitants presently set themselves in battle against each other. As I continued looking at the bright angel, on whose brow rested a crown of light on which was traced the word "Union," I saw the angel place an American flag between the divided nation, and say, "Remember, ye are brethren." Instantly, the inhabitants, casting from them their weapons, became friends once more, and united around the National Standard.

After this vision, another of yet later times came into view, preceded once more by the fateful injunction, "Son of the Republic, look and learn." This time the angelic being took water from the ocean and cast it over Europe, Asia, and Africa. From these continents, hordes of armed men came over America, devastating the country. Another time the angel cast water upon America, and clouds and armies drew back, giving victory to the country. Once again, cities and towns blossomed anew, and the angel proclaimed, "While the stars remain in the heaven and send down dew upon the earth, so long shall the union last."

The vision started to dissolve, but before taking its leave, the angelic visitor instructed the general, "Son of the Republic, what you have just seen is thus interpreted: Three great perils will come upon the Republic. The most fearful is the third; but the whole world united shall not prevail against her." Washington, recollecting the whole, summed up the experience in this way: "[I] felt I had seen a vision wherein had been shown to me the birth, progress, and destiny of the United States." Washington entrusted the entire story of his vision at Valley Forge to his aide, Anthony Sherman, who took abundant notes at the time. It was later published in the December 1880 issue of the *National Tribune*.

There is another individual who towered in stature equal to Washington, and that is Benjamin Franklin. In his mind, the idea of a union of the colonies lived long before it could come to realization. Franklin, too, was a first one, one of those rare individuals whom a nation encounters at a significant turning point in its genesis or history. And his spirituality made him a pioneer not only in America, but the world over.

Benjamin Franklin's Unique Spirituality

Benjamin Franklin's life encompassed practically the whole of the eighteenth century. Many of the tendencies living in the century found a significant representative in Franklin. However, he was unlike most (if not all) of his contemporaries, in that for him the roads of science and religion never separated. Thus for him the term *philosophy*, equivalent to knowledge or science, stood for both natural and moral philosophy. Chief among his concerns was the social world. To understand what made Franklin unique, we need to look at two major tendencies at play in eighteenth-century religion.

Religious and political freedoms were perceived as indivisibly linked in Franklin's time. At that time, religion was very much alive in American society. No single denomination constituted a majority throughout the colonies. This condition helped create an atmosphere of religious tolerance. Whereas dissent from the established church involved only an estimated 7 percent in England, it was the daily reality for two thirds of the colonials.[14] Churches often elected lay elders to operate in the absence of mandated clergy. Thus, from the very beginning and for the most varied reasons, church attendance had a voluntary character. The various denominations sidestepped many organizational obstacles by choosing leaders from the laity and forming congregations at will, thereby increasing their popular appeal.

Many churchgoers cared little for doctrine, often choosing affiliations according to proximity and convenience. Therefore, there was fluidity between faiths. The issues influencing religious affiliation were often social rather than ideological. Churches provided much of the colonial education, assured assistance to the poor, and created societies for women and youth. In this fluid situation, two new streams developed from traditional religion. One would later be called evangelical, the other liberal.

The evangelical movement was the offspring of the Great Awakening, a religious stirring that swept over America, culminating in the years 1739 to 1745. Central to its message was the experience of conversion or salvation, which was characterized by a strong personal element. The evangelicals wanted to move toward a simpler creed of the heart. Compared with the traditional clergy, the evangelicals were either

American-born or had emigrated early in life. The traditionalists were nearly all educated abroad.

From another direction came the liberal movement, a reflection of the ideas of the enlightenment as they had been developed in Europe, mostly by English and French philosophers such as Voltaire, Rousseau, Algernon, Sidney, and Locke. The ideas that expressed themselves mainly through political channels in Europe found easy acceptance within the American congregations. Whereas the evangelicals appealed to the new dogma of salvation, the liberals stripped religious creed of all but the bare essentials. What they professed was a natural religion. In practice, a new faith without dogma, often also devoid of substance, parted ways with the scientific outlook.

When the rebellion began, the religious dividing lines proved of no consequence in the matter of loyalties to revolution or crown. The revolution found strong support among the clergy. The development of religious ideas reflected a conspicuous difference between the American experience and the sociopolitical conditions in Europe. America had no feudal heritage and no strongly established church hierarchy. The clergy was not compromised by ties with the British government. The situation in Europe had often brought about a strong polarization around religious matters: religious orthodoxy on one hand, antireligious feelings on the other. That was particularly the case in France, where the Catholic religion was part of the system of oppression.

Something new, however, was on the horizon: a personal way to reach spiritual conviction, a spirituality of individuality and experience, supported by science; and its proponent was a young printer from Philadelphia. In his groundbreaking approach, we recognize seeds that further germinated in the American soul, seeds that find new forms even at present. In this prophetic soul, a spirituality of faith (conservative) and of science (liberal) were reconciled.

Before age twenty-one, the young printer had already left behind the rigorous Puritanism of Boston. In his autobiography, he revealed that at age fifteen he started doubting biblical revelation, and at age twenty-four he practically abandoned attendance at Sunday worship. Contrary to his contemporaries, his rejection of dogma did not lead him toward the purely rationalistic outlook of the liberals. He was only twenty-two when he wrote his *Articles of Belief and Acts of Religion*, which included themes of adoration, petition, and duty. It was, in effect, an equivalent of a personal daily worship. At age twenty-four, Franklin was proposing a United Party for Virtue, or more expressively, The Society of the Free and Easy, by "forming the virtuous and good men of all nations into a regular body, to be governed by suitable, good, and wise rules."

In reviewing the philosopher's ideas, we may come to define what Franklin calls the Art of Virtue, the book he never managed to write. Franklin's art of virtue is right action: "For doing the good, to me, is the only service in our power; and to imitate His beneficences is to glorify Him."

Right action is subordinated to right thinking. "Evil as evil can never be chosen," he reminds us, "and though evil is often the effect of our own choice, yet we never desire it but under the appearance of ordinary good." Thus, although right thinking, as the prerequisite to good action, sounds simple, in reality it is not. Its main enemy is passion, which allows us to appreciate only the consequences of the immediate present, not those that follow. Reason lets us perceive both the immediate and future effects of our deeds. However, reason alone is not sufficient, for it can be obscured by pride and ambition. Therefore, to be able to use reason as a tool of discernment, we must be able to conduct a dispassionate self-analysis.

At an early stage of his life, Franklin gave this self-analysis the form of the thirteen virtues (temperance, order, silence, resolution, frugality, industry, sincerity, justice, moderation, cleanliness, tranquility, chastity, and humility). According to the method that he devised, he practiced each virtue a week at a time. In a year, the whole set of virtues could be practiced exactly four times. Naively intended as a device for attaining perfection, the system became for Franklin a tool for self-awareness, showing him his weaknesses and promoting personal improvement. Through such a devised procedure, Franklin became a modern scientist of inner development, endeavoring to observe himself, much in the way he would later observe electricity. This personal way of testing himself and acknowledging his own errors and shortcomings led Franklin to an independent view of morality. He called it "moral algebra," a way of weighing the pros and cons of his deeds and taking time before making important decisions. Franklin was thus breaking the ground for a new vision of morality, one no longer dictated by religion or external moral precepts, but by individual consciousness.

Franklin's religion (his own form of spirituality) was intimately personal, and to quite a degree scientific, rather than merely rational; it stemmed from very new and unprecedented ideas, such as the ability to look at the inner life with scientific objectivity. His central message, "let conscience be your guide," would be taken further and refined by Emerson in the next century.

Washington became a living embodiment of the art of virtue that was Franklin's ambition. The young nation owed to Washington the fact that it became a republic; had Washington not been able to curb his not-inconsiderable ambition, he would have most naturally coveted the power offered to him and clung to it. It is in such moments of history that the biography of a pivotal individual and that of a nation are completely interwoven with each other.

Other forces played a part in the birth of the nation, in addition to the ones portrayed in a syncretistic way by Tamanend. These will be discussed in the next chapter.

Chapter 2

From Longhouse and Lodge:
The Dream of Equality

Thy word is good, but a word is nothing until it is given form and sent
to work in the world. What form shall the message take when it comes
to dwell among men?
　　　　　—*The White Roots of Peace* (Paul A. W. Wallace version)

When I arrived in Pennsylvania in April 1996, I had just finished
reading Bruce Johansen's seminal work *Forgotten Founders*, chronicling
the remarkable achievements of Iroquois polity and the influence of
the longhouse (Haudenosaunee) over the resolve of the colonies to seek
independence and form a federal compact. One day I was reading Nancy
Bonvillain's brief retelling of the legend of *The White Roots of Peace*.[1]
Immediately I had an inner reaction: *This is even more important than
what the Iroquois achieved*, or rather, *This explains why the Iroquois
revolution was much more than the adoption of amazing social structures
and why it endured as long as it did*. And I felt that knowing the legend
would be as important, or more important, than knowing what the
Iroquois achieved outwardly. When I realized this, I looked for every
possible version of the story. I wanted to capture all the shades of
meaning that would be present in some renderings and not in others,
and have a comprehensive understanding of the whole. This quest was
based on the understanding that legends offer images and that different
versions of the same legends offer different images that add meaning,
enrich, and complement each other. That proved to be true.

　　The American republic, or federal system of government, was born
in a place where federalism already had a long tradition. The previous
chapter mentioned the Lenni-Lenape federation, along with the influence

that the Tamanend ideal had on the colonists. Many confederacies of native tribes existed along the Atlantic coast of North America; all of them originally had a semifeudal character. The recognized sachem, or leader, received tributes from the various tribes and pledges of allegiance, such as a sovereign king would receive from his vassals. In return, the vassals received protection against common enemies.

The Iroquois League: The Message and the Form

The Iroquois League unites five nations and represents a radical departure from all previous models. It was the first confederation of equal nations and did not rest on the idea of monarchy. The Five Nations' Confederacy traces its origin to the historical legend of *The White Roots of Peace.*

Some modern authors have claimed that the ideas put forth by the Iroquois served as a blueprint for the American Constitution. The proof brought forth is very eloquent, but not conclusive. It rests primarily on Benjamin Franklin's relationship with the Five Nations and his knowledge of their traditions. Although the Iroquois League was a key influence in the birth of the American federal system, it is obviously not the only one. The colonists also had a long tradition of compacts and constitutions hearkening back to Anglo-Saxon tradition. We need not invoke a link of causality between two such different societies as the Iroquois and the American. It is the Iroquois social construct—its spiritual underpinnings detectable in the legend—rather than its political structure that lives and plunges its roots into the American Revolution and the Declaration of Independence. Therefore it is significant that Benjamin Franklin acknowledged that outlook and that it later played such a prominent role in the formation of the American ideal.

The Iroquois, as they were called by the French, occupied the northern portion of present-day New York State in a territory extending roughly between the Genesee and Hudson Rivers. The Confederacy comprised the five tribes of Senecas, Cayugas, Onondagas, Oneidas, and Mohawks. The symbol of their legend, the tree of the white roots, stands for *peace* in the larger sense of the word, a peace that in their language corresponds with law—in other words, sacred law.

The events related in the legend of *The White Roots of Peace* occurred between 1400 and 1500, most likely around 1450. However, some methods of dating place the founding of the league at an earlier stage, some two centuries before. There are many versions of this historical legend. The accuracy of the sources relating the events varies according to the kind of witnesses recording them and the time of these recordings. Some versions are obviously shorter renderings trimmed of any legendary character and made fit for a more modern, rational ear. The most noticeable variations lie in the identification of Hiawatha and Deganawidah in one single individual, Hiawatha, and the deletion of the virgin birth. Of all the versions known, I will refer mainly to Paul Wallace's retelling, taken from three different sources at the turn of the nineteenth century. Wallace was a thorough interpreter of Iroquois culture and was completely immersed in their way of thinking. We will occasionally use other sources to amplify Wallace's version.

The Legend of the White Roots of Peace

Deganawidah, the central hero of the history, was born among the Huron, a tribe on the north shore of Lake Ontario. He was a foreigner, not from the Five Nations. He was the son of a virgin, and his name, meaning "Master of Things," was revealed to his grandmother by an appearance of the Great Spirit. Deganawidah's declared mission was to bring peace and spread what he called the "new mind" among the nations. He wanted to turn his back on war and revenge and bring about a new law. Although he was an exalted being, Deganawidah had a stutter.

When Deganawidah had grown to manhood, he set out toward the rising sun, riding in a white canoe made of stone, knowing that he would not return. He arrived on the southern shore of Lake Ontario in Iroquois territory, which at that time was ravaged by strife, and went from one settlement to another spreading the word of peace. After visiting these settlements, Deganawidah went to the house of a woman "who lived by the warrior's path that passed between the east and west." To the woman Deganawidah recited the message of peace, which he divided into three parts: *righteousness*, the desire to see justice embodied; *health*, meaning harmony of body and mind, the foundation for peace; and *power*, based on law that has the backing of force, but a force that translates the desire of the "holder of the heavens."

To answer the woman's question of which form this message would take in the world, Deganawidah foretold what would later be known as the longhouse, "the house of many fires," symbol of a confederacy of equals. The woman embraced the message, and Deganawidah gave her the name *Jigonhsasee,* meaning the "New Face that Embodies the New Mind," and told her that she would be remembered as "Mother of Nations."

Upon leaving the woman, Deganawidah proceeded toward the sunrise, knowing that he would have to meet with "the man who eats humans" in Onondaga territory. Arriving at the Onondaga chief's hut, Deganawidah climbed on the roof and stood waiting, with his head next to the smoke hole. The man returned home with a corpse and set the kettle over the fire. On the surface of the water, he saw Deganawidah's face, and he believed it to be his own reflection. Detecting in it a strength and wisdom that he had never imagined before, he started questioning his cannibalistic habits. This change of mind brought him sorrow at the realization of the evil he had committed. Thus moved, he pondered what needed to be done in order to compensate for the pain he had caused. At that moment, Deganawidah entered the hut, appearing to the man. The latter related his experience, and Deganawidah offered him the means of redressing his wrongs by explaining to him the "Good News of Peace and Power." From then on, the cannibal would have the name *Hiawatha* (which means "he who combs"). At the same time, he was given the task and challenge of enlisting the wizard Atotarho to their cause.

Atotarho, whose name means "entangled," was versed in the arts of magic. He had "a twisted body and a twisted mind, and his hair was a mass of tangled snakes." He struck terror in his enemies and held great power. His cry *"Hwe-do-ne-e-e-e-e-eh,"* meaning "When shall this be?" was said to be "the mocking cry of the doubter who killed men by destroying their faith." He could strike his enemies even at great distances. Before setting Hiawatha on his new task, Deganawidah visited the wizard and announced to him the coming of the good news of peace and power, without managing to sway his mind. Still proceeding toward the sunrise, he arrived among the last Iroquois tribe, the Mohawks. They were favorably inclined toward the message, but wanted to receive a sign by testing the messenger.

They asked the foreigner to climb a tree next to the lower falls of the Mohawk River. They felled the tree over the river, and Deganawidah survived into the next day, unscathed. This was the sign they desired, and the Mohawks accepted the prophet's message. They were the first nation to accept the new mind.

Following his master, Hiawatha arrived in Onondaga territory. There he spread the new message without managing to loosen Atotarho's grip over his people's minds. Three times he called a council, and after each one of them, one of his daughters fell ill and died, victim of the powers of Atotarho. Finally, the Onondagas arranged to have a game of lacrosse performed to lift Hiawatha's spirits. During the game, a mysterious bird came down from heaven. The crowd pursuing the bird caused the death of Hiawatha's wife, who was trampled in the onrush. Unable to contain his grief, Hiawatha wandered away toward the east. He reached one of the Tully Lakes; there the ducks lifted the water to give him a dry passage. On the bottom of the lake, he found shells that he strung together with three ropes. Those he set on a horizontal pole supported by two vertical ones. Holding each string in turn, Hiawatha recited words of comfort, which he pledged to repeat to anyone who mourns over a loss. This is the origin of the so-called ritual of condolence. In vain he waited for anyone to console him. After a few weeks of mourning, he arrived at the village by the lower falls of the Mohawk River. There he reconnected with Deganawidah. The master relieved Hiawatha of his grief by repeating the very same ritual of condolence.

At this point, Deganawidah and Hiawatha set out to complete their task by concretely envisioning the form that they wanted to give to their message of peace. One after another, the tribes accepted their message. The final obstacle was Atotarho. The two decided that Deganawidah would sing to him the song of peace, while Hiawatha would explain the words of the law. They set forth in a canoe across a lake to meet Atotarho. The wizard, using his last magic powers, sent winds and waves against the canoe, but to no avail. Deganawidah and Hiawatha thus brought their message to a skeptical, but more receptive, Atotarho.

To accomplish the great reconciliation he had in mind, Deganawidah invested Atotarho with the highest authority over the Five Nations. In the presence of the Five Nations, he told Atotarho: "Behold! Here is Power. These are the Five Nations. Their strength is greater than your strength. But their voice shall be your voice when thou speak in council, and all men shall hear you." Then Atotarho's mind was made straight, and Hiawatha combed the snakes out of his hair (hence the meaning of Hiawatha's name). Deganawidah laid his hands on the wizard's body and removed the seven crooks. Then he placed antlers on Atotarho's and the other chiefs' heads, as a symbol of their new authority.

The implications of this legend, and the historical events that ensued, are a rich mine of truth and inspiration. In the language of the legend, the new mind must bring about a new form. New ideas shape a new reality in the social world.

Deganawidah and Hiawatha

In most versions of the legend, Hiawatha and Deganawidah formed a duality. Occasionally they merged into the single individuality of Hiawatha. The dynamic of the legend revolves around the two of them and Atotarho.

Deganawidah's biography is by far the most extraordinary of the three, since he was conceived by a virgin. In some versions of the legend, the messenger also prophesied that Deganawidah would indirectly bring the downfall of his people, the Hurons. The grandmother tried to kill him by throwing him in the freezing waters, and twice again in unspecified ways.[2]

In Deganawidah, we see a prophet who came to introduce new spiritual principles. That he was a highly evolved individual is indicated by the fact that he rode in a white canoe made of stone. In the version of the legend quoted above, once his mission was accomplished, Deganawidah rowed in his canoe toward the setting sun, never to be seen again. In the version given by Horatio Hale, it is said that Deganawidah was the only name that was not used down through the line of heredity, in contrast to the names of all the other chiefs who were present at the foundation of the league. This is because none can do what he did.[3]

30

Like Deganawidah, Atotarho shared a mixture of human and superhuman attributes. His cry was "the mocking cry of the doubter who killed men by destroying their faith." The translation of the cry means, "When shall this be?" This impatient attitude is typical of a being who wants events to emerge before their time. The physical appearance of Atotarho (his crooked body, his head covered with snakes) is the expression of the fact that he was a black magician.

Hiawatha stood between these two extremes. His flaw, cannibalism, was a major trespass inherited as a cultural habit. It was a practice tied to war and religious beliefs. Cannibalism stood at the center of the encounter between Hiawatha and Deganawidah. Because Hiawatha was in touch with his true humanity, he was able to overcome his cannibalistic habit. The prophet allowed him to recognize his shortcomings and realize his full human potential. This brought about the recognition of the pain caused to others and the desire to redeem himself, made possible by Deganawidah's message.

Soon after, Hiawatha took on the task of helping his people. The length of the process of grief is emphasized by the establishment of the ritual of condolence, the burdensome journey to the Mohawk nation, and the earnest desire to bring consolation to others. Only Deganawidah knew the depth of Hiawatha's sorrow. He could reach to the spiritual source, which offered Hiawatha peace and allowed for perception of the truth that suffering had obscured.

The dynamic of development moving between the two founders shows significant nuances that could escape a superficial examination. Hiawatha was as much a pupil of Deganawidah as he was a collaborator. Although the prophet carried the vision, he was also impaired by his stuttering. He needed someone else with oratorical skills; that was Hiawatha's role. Although Deganawidah guided and inspired, it was Hiawatha who carried out the burden of the central confrontation with Atotarho. Hiawatha could not make use of supernatural powers, as Deganawidah did in the instance of the test of the fallen tree. Still, it was Hiawatha who established the ritual of condolence and who combed Atotarho's hair. The prophet Deganawidah had to find a willing companion before he could realize his mission. With the achievement of the league, Deganawidah's task came to an end. Hiawatha still had a political task to carry out.

What Can the Legend Teach Us Now?

Human beings are surrounded by their particular cultural context. Hiawatha, an early Iroquois chief, was born into a society that practiced cannibalism and some other forms of ritual magic for the sake of gaining power over others.

The Path of Personal Transformation

Hiawatha's encounter with the prophet was one of those exceptional events in a lifetime, a defining moment. Hiawatha was struck by the countenance of the Peacemaker and convinced by his message, which caused him to reassess his life, and he resolved to rebuild it upon the new values of righteousness, health, and power imparted by the prophet. What was unusual in Hiawatha was the depth of his turnaround and the earnestness with which he embraced and embodied the message. Change was inevitable; there was no going back. And what did it mean to go forward?

A naïve assumption takes for granted the power of utopian ideals to shape a new future with perfect justice and freedom for all. Historically, this has never been accomplished. Modern attempts at utopia have simply led to bloodshed and horrors, from the French Revolution to Russian Communism or German Nazism. What the legend of *The White Roots of Peace* illustrates is quite different. Only a simplistic modern perspective could assume that as soon as Hiawatha embraced the message, suddenly it was just a matter of organizing the right committees and implementing the right decisions. The legend has more depth and wisdom than that. When something new comes on the horizon, the established order reacts and puts it to the test. Atotarho, the wizened magician, had more than one arrow to his bow, and he did not hesitate to use them. As soon as Hiawatha acted within the new mind, Atotarho reacted. The deaths of all Hiawatha's immediate family followed. The violent reaction failed to take into account the power of new ideas rooted in the spirit.

Hiawatha was not yet ready to further the message of social renewal; like all civilizing heroes, he had to undergo tests. As a chief and a cannibal, he knew what it was to impart suffering to others. Now he was on the receiving end. And an important inner journey of transformation and personal redemption began.

Hiawatha wandered aimlessly, to all outward appearance. In reality, the act of resisting the inner urge for vengeance, although not visible to the external world, appearing as something purely passive, is the most intense spiritual activity. The legend tells us that no one could approach Hiawatha and bring him consolation, because no one knew of such suffering. The prophet could have consoled him, but he was waiting for Hiawatha's transformation to reach completion. And Hiawatha did accomplish a remarkable metamorphosis, but only when the time was ripe. In a beautiful image, we are told of how his grief was lifted. What appeared impossible (crossing the lake on foot) was made possible by the ducks lifting the water for him. What seemed impossible (the overcoming of such a crushing grief as Hiawatha's) was made possible by the depth to which the message had penetrated the chief's soul and by the suffering he was willing to bear for it. This is a message that a modern political activist often does not want to hear. This is what made Hiawatha's deed one that lives on; centuries later, it still carries a civilizing impulse.

After Hiawatha crossed the dry lake bed on foot, he picked up the wampum shells, placed them on three strings, and created the ritual of condolence. Hiawatha truly and completely processed his grief; he saw the larger purpose of it. Only someone undergoing a transformation of this magnitude could understand the grief that his people had gone through for centuries because of decadent cultural practices.

What follows is remarkable. The prophet was there to perform the ritual of condolence because Hiawatha had removed all the inner obstacles and made it possible. Nothing could now possibly stop the strength of the two men. When they presented themselves to the tyrant, he could only play his last tricks; to be sure, they were formidable feats. No one is in the position of Atotarho unless he knows something, possesses knowledge that could be used for the good but that he has decided to use for his own advantage. Atotarho was a "wise man," but the negative image of the Peacemaker. One man used his knowledge selflessly to liberate his fellow human beings; the other, gripped by fear, used power to further his own goals. The story shows that the Peacemaker knew of the perverted wisdom of Atotarho.

Now to the epilogue. Decadent social practices do not exist in a vacuum; there are the perpetrators and the enablers. Without the enablers, the Atotarhos of this world would have nowhere to go. When decadent social practices have persisted for a long time, there is a culture that pervades and masks all values; common sense has been turned upside down. Well-meaning reformers can alter surface appearances for a short time, but nothing will really change until culture is affected. Hiawatha tapped into what can be called cultural power. Culture is the realm where identities (of individuals, groups, and nations) are forged. New identities must be created that are powerful enough to transform every facet of the economy, polity, and the culture itself. The greatest cultural heroes are spiritual and moral leaders (we saw one in George Washington).

Hiawatha acquired new inner powers. He inwardly overcame the force that Atotarho used outwardly to divide and conquer. As long as the tribes were at each other's throats, Atotarho had an easy task. As long as they preferred to nurse factional interests instead of the interests of the whole, isolated actions from individual tribes could do nothing against the power of Atotarho, the power that paralyzed faith through the cry "Hwe-do-ne-e-e-e-eh" (When shall this be?). Together with the Peacemaker, Hiawatha could offer new inner certainty to the tribes. The Peacemaker alone could never have reached this goal; after all, he was not even one of the Iroquois people. But an Iroquois fully embraced the new mind and embodied it; a formidable task was brought to its completion.

Aligning the Personal and the Political

The representatives of the Five Nations must have sensed that something was different in Hiawatha. Perhaps they saw how aligned the Peacemaker and Hiawatha were with each other. Their customary thinking would have led them to believe that a chief who did not against the violence inflicted upon him would be "less than a man." What was Hiawatha hoping to prove by letting Atotarho's crime go unrevenged? Now the Iroquois could begin to fathom a new cultural precedent, which they did not yet fully understand. The two men were truly more powerful than Atotarho, even without resorting to violence.

The tribes together summoned the courage to face the magician of the land. And the magician tried his last tricks, which no longer worked. The magician's power lay in dividing. Now that the tribes had been united, he could not stand up to so much strength, and he no longer had a hold over people's minds.

The Peacemaker, however, has some surprises in store for us. There was a better future in store even for Atotarho. He, too, would be part of the new social order, but first he needed healing. And that is the unprecedented message of the prophet. He intended to inaugurate not only a different political compact, but also a different way of looking at retribution and punishment. About Atotarho, the prophet said earlier, "He is evil, but we need him." What greater wisdom lies behind this statement? In some legends, it is shown that Atotarho was a magician who had a choice and took the wrong path, which led him downhill. He could have been an equal to the Peacemaker had he mustered the necessary inner strength. But the Peacemaker, because he had a deeper knowledge of human nature, knew that Atotarho could still be redeemed. This is why he invested Atotarho with the highest ceremonial role.

It is true that before taking this unprecedented step, the Peacemaker had healed Atotarho; he had removed the seven crooks from his body and the snakes from his hair, with the help of Hiawatha. Deganawidah knew that all craving for power and dominion over others signals an illness of the soul. Such knowledge allowed him to have compassion for the very real suffering of Atotarho. The oppressor cannot really be a happy person, but very few can understand the plight of such a one; fewer still will help the oppressor. Political and economic oppression is carried not only outwardly through instruments of domination; it is also reproduced in our thinking, our feelings, and our habits. We need to meet it within as much as we find it externally in society. Deganawidah knew this when he entrusted his mission to a cannibal. Why would he have looked at Atotarho any differently than Hiawatha?

We are coming to the end of the story. Atotarho had been healed and the Peacemaker's mission had come to an end, but Hiawatha's mission was really just beginning. But the legend has still other implications on the social level. The ritual of condolence was given a central place in Iroquois society, although this is not immediately noticeable in the legend. Before the advent of the league, the strife between the tribes was perpetuated by cycles of war and revenge, cannibalism, and black magic. The new cornerstone of Iroquois society then became recognition of the need for the process of grief and condolence to replace the cycle of violence and revenge. The ritual of condolence made possible the harmonization of the aims of the community by allowing individuals to overcome their grief and align their goals with those of others. Grief is seen as a veil covering the senses and the heart. The ritual of condolence lifts these veils and makes explicit the second principle expressed by Deganawidah: health as harmony between spirit and body.

More important still is the outcome of the legend in the form of government that arose within the Iroquois community. The new word was the message of justice, health, and power. The Iroquois knew that a word is nothing without a form. They embodied the word in the form of the longhouse (Haudenosaunee), symbolizing the union of many fires, which stood for the idea of confederacy. For the first time, nations stood as equals, no more as vassals. Authority was defined by complex organizational levels built to ensure that no individual, or single nation, could at any time impose their will upon the community. Political power was also clearly differentiated from religious power. It was, in fact, a system of checks and balances, obliging the representatives of power to seek broad consensus in all their decisions. More detail about this form of government can be found in the fine analysis by Bruce Johansen.[4]

The Iroquois achievement is incredibly significant. It prepared a favorable ground specifically in the eastern part of the North American continent, where the American federal government saw its birth.

A New Look at the American Revolution:
Franklin and Washington

In the light shed by the previous examination of European and Native American influences, the process of the American Revolution and gaining independence reveals several threads weaving within the otherwise well-known events. We will focus on two levels. The first is the dynamic of the events, which shows how the Iroquois impulse was alive under the surface. More easily seen, but often misunderstood, is the contribution of early Freemasonry. Two extreme views hold the ground about Freemasonry. One view almost completely dismisses Freemasonry and tends to minimize, if not obliterate, its part in the events leading to the birth of the federal government. The other view sees a hidden Freemason conspiracy. The facts tend to prove something different from either of the two extremes. Little-known and unexplored facts reveal a different image of the familiar events.

The Ethos of Freemasonry

The development of modern Freemasonry is intimately intertwined with the Scottish monarchy, the Stuarts in particular, and later with the English monarchy after the unification of the two kingdoms.[5] Scottish Masonry was the repository of the true origin of Freemasonry and included the so-called higher grades, leading to the Royal Arch, and tended on the whole to be a less elitist movement. The English Grand Lodge, on the other hand, had a profound influence on the thought of the enlightened reformers of the eighteenth century: Hume, Locke, Voltaire, Diderot, Montesquieu, and Rousseau. Some of them were Freemasons, while others were influenced by the prevailing Freemasonic ideas.

Freemasonry acted upon society as a social solvent. In England it contributed greatly to the breakdown of the rigid social class system. For example, Jews were admitted into Freemasonry and public life in England earlier than elsewhere in Europe. Freemasonry also contributed to the distinction between man and office, so necessary to the development and furtherance of all democratic institutions.

An important development of Freemasonry was its spread throughout Ireland. There the early Scottish Masonry preserved aspects that had been lost in England. It was the Irish lodges that granted charters to the so-called field lodges of the British Army. Through these, Freemasonry spread over to the New World. The division between Freemasonry of English origin and of Scottish origin was mirrored in America between the Moderns (English Freemasonry) and the Ancients (Scottish Freemasonry). The first lodges were those of the Moderns. Philadelphia had its own St. John Lodge in 1730, to which Benjamin Franklin belonged. A humble printer, having no special claim by birth, Franklin had already become grand master by that time. The Moderns started to decline around the 1740s, while the Ancients were on the rise. Philadelphia's first Ancient lodge was formed in 1757. The difference between the two lay in the centralism expected by the English lodge, contrasted with the broad independence maintained by the Scottish or Irish lodges. Once formed, the latter lodges tended to lose contact with the sponsoring body. A Freemasonry that was more politically independent and closer to its origin, together with religious denominations exerting wide degrees of freedom, no doubt contributed to allow in the colonies a much larger cultural independence than was possible anywhere in Europe.

Together with rituals, Freemasonry introduced a strong social ethic. This began with the rules of etiquette. These rules included the salute between members, the admission to the lodge (which required unanimous agreement following scrutiny of the moral character of the candidate), and such seemingly mundane things as dining and singing together. Controversial topics were banned from the gatherings. Moreover, a whole code of conduct, celebrating moral virtue and fraternal love, was promoted within the brotherhood.

It may not at first be apparent how such values could derive from the ancient craft guilds. In order to perceive this, we must look at what the crafts achieved in the realm of morality. As long as the organization of labor in the crafts survived, the human being's intimate connection with vocation and the fruit of one's labor also persisted. This connection would subsequently be lost with the dawn of the age of industrialization, which saw a progressive specialization and division of labor. With these changes came a separation between the human being and the fruits of his or her work.

All crafts required that the apprentice learn many specific gestures. The craft gesture is different from machine labor because it preserves the personal interaction of the worker with the material used. Through these particular gestures, the crafts allowed a specific training of the will. The gestures had specific rhythms, which had to be acquired gradually and then individualized. In this sense, they deeply influenced human morality.

Doing the good, acting in the sphere of morality, was the inheritance from the craft guilds within Freemasonry. The relation to the craft materials and aims then extended to relationships within the fellowship. There were three things that the apprentice had to forgo: gratuitous curiosity, the fear to acknowledge his or her own failings and mistakes, and the inability to rise in spirit above all things that differentiate one human being from another. In this we see why original Freemasonry could accept all religious and political ideas. Its universal tolerance enabled it to transcend and unite them in spirit.

The role of Freemasonry in America was made possible by the social and spiritual climate that pervaded the colonies in the eighteenth century, a spirit quite different from its European counterpart. This unique spirit was enhanced by the stature of many great individuals— and some truly exceptional ones. We have examined the individuality of Washington. Behind him, the figure of the nearly forgotten spiritual father of America, Benjamin Franklin, looms even larger. Through the complementary actions of these two towering individuals, the early Freemason impulse of Scotland and the Iroquois impulse converged into a first tentative experiment of social art on a national level. These interlocking influences played their part in the American form of government.

The New Message

We have already seen what a special position Franklin occupied in the scientific and spiritual thinking of his time. We can say he was a lone exception to the unavoidable tendency of the era, which tended to polarize science and religion. Franklin showed the way to an experiential spirituality that would be devoid of dogma, an inner perception of morality that upholds a free and completely individual path. This path led him to experiment with thirteen virtues, to assess the effects of both consumption and abstention from alcohol and meat, and to determine how right thinking could lead him to right action. But Franklin's role was not limited to the depth of his speculative thinking. As early as 1764, he was appropriately called the "first American."[6] (The term was later transferred to Washington. It is easy to see why Washington, the man of action, could usurp the title.) Even so, America was an idea before it became a political task, and in that sense the honor belongs to Franklin. We will examine the main aspects of Franklin's life before moving on to list his contributions to the founding of the new nation.

Franklin, like Washington, had been groomed in the American school of business, but unlike Washington, his was an enterprise of the written word. His mission was to spread the word not only in America, but also to the world. By age forty-two, both men had reached prominent places in their society, north and south. At that age, they had achieved a high degree of economic independence and could devote their endeavors to the commonwealth.

Both Washington and Franklin had strong physical constitutions. However, Franklin was more than twenty years older than the Virginian and had a very different character. Whereas the young Washington towered in ambition, the young Franklin tended to naiveté. His childhood friend John Collins squandered the money that Franklin had collected for his employer, a Mr. Vernon, and this left the young Franklin in debt. Later, William Keith, governor of Pennsylvania, sent Franklin on a mission to London, but did not send him with proper support. In London, the story repeated itself; Franklin's friend James Ralph lived at Franklin's expense. This was not the last episode, but by then, Franklin had learned not to be so naïve. His amiability, brightness, and constant striving toward self-improvement quickly compensated for other personality flaws.

Whereas Washington could bring the essence of the American experience within his reach through his enormous will, Franklin attained the same end through his travels and his interactions with people and ideas. During his visit to France in 1767, he wrote to his friend Polly Stevenson: "Traveling is one way of strengthening life, at least in appearance. It is but a fortnight since we left London, but the variety of scenes we have gone through makes it equal to six months living in one place. Perhaps I have suffered a greater change, too, in my person, than I could have done in six years at home."

The Education of Benjamin Franklin

In his early youth, Franklin was already a leader among his peers in their games. He had a yearning toward the ocean, which he associated with the idea of wanting to sail. In that we can see an intimation of his destiny, which took him across the ocean to Europe. In his adolescent years, he had unusual preoccupations with moral and spiritual matters, as he showed in his experiments with abstention from meat and alcohol. These were existential questions that the young man wanted to explore through his own experience.

His transition into adulthood around the age of twenty-one was fraught with many intense trials. In London he had contacted a group of young radical freethinkers and set out to prove "in a hundred axioms that he knew neither sin, nor liberty, nor personal immortality. God was only permitted to exist as a machine." He returned to Philadelphia feeling that he could have fallen into an abyss. Another abyss followed, one in which he almost lost his life after an attack of pleurisy. His friend and mentor Thomas Denham actually died from the illness they had contracted together. Of the depth of this experience, we can gather some insight from his own words: "I suffered a good deal, gave up the point in my mind, and was rather disappointed when I found myself recovering; regretting in some degree that I must now some time or other have all that disagreeable work to do over again."

That Franklin gained a glimpse into the spiritual world seems beyond doubt. The next year he composed the famous epitaph in which he said the following about his corpse: "for it will (as he believ'd) Appear once More in a New and More Elegant Edition Revised and Corrected by the Author." What has not been sufficiently highlighted about this turning point is that Franklin had a very deep spiritual experience. In present-day parlance, we could say he had a near-death experience and may even have awakened some dim memory of a previous life.

Thoughtful examination of the evidence reveals an already exceptional individual, now fully awakened through the power of the spirit to his life calling, and to tasks that were far from ordinary.

The spiritual experience had awakened astonishing insights for a man of the eighteenth century, insights coming from inner conviction rather than from borrowed knowledge. This was also the time in which Franklin formed the *Junto,* or Leather Apron Club, a club for mutual improvement, where he and his friends debated questions of science, morality, politics, and business. Four years before becoming a Freemason, Franklin had started this group, which shared much of its philosophy with the brotherhood. His later affiliation with Freemasonry formed a thread throughout his whole life.

A glimpse at what Franklin's mind could encompass is truly astonishing. We can look first at the speculative sciences. Franklin's discoveries about electricity are all the more remarkable considering that he had little equipment and gave little time to his experiments. His insights endure today in the definition of positive and negative fields. More astonishing but little-known is Franklin's mathematical genius. Through his friendship with the statesman and natural scientist James Logan, Franklin had become acquainted with mathematical magic squares. These are square tables of eight columns by eight rows filled with seemingly random numbers. The sum of each column or row as well as the diagonals yield the same constant number. Not only could Franklin replicate such squares on his own; he could also add a host of additional constant properties to the 8 x 8 squares and also do the same with 16 x 16 squares.[7] We can note in passing that everything that Franklin touched is far from ordinary. He discovered electricity almost like one would work on a hobby, and he could work at magic squares in his amateur fashion, but much in the way as trained mathematicians would. There seems to be hardly a limit to his genius.

Thus, Franklin's mind could have excelled in speculative pursuits. On the other hand, Franklin's pursuit of knowledge led to many practical applications. His practical achievements may seem less impressive than the ones we just mentioned, but they had an immediate benefit for his community and the whole of the colonies. With the printing press, he worked his way into his fellow citizens' minds through *Poor Richard's*

Almanac. This condensed wisdom, summed up in a few words and peppered with humor, was particularly adapted to the ways of the New World. His declared intention was to "leave a strong impression on the memory of young persons."[8]

Franklin's very approach toward knowledge is a radical departure from the ways of the academic world. His Leather Apron Club or *Junto* is a model of learning achieved in lively collaboration, the knowledge accessible to the leather-apron man, that is, to the craftsman, and by extension, to all. Franklin understood that we learn from active interchange, and from life as much as from academic study. It is through the agency of the *Junto* that the Lending Library, the City Watch, and the American Philosophical Society were born. About the improvements brought by the City Watch, Franklin said: "by preparing the minds of the people for the change, it paved the way for the law obtained a few years later, when the members of our clubs were grown into more influence." Here we see another of Franklin's capacities, the one that early Freemasonry stressed: the ability to guide through deeds, deliberately relinquishing ownership of the ideas. This implies the willingness to plant a seed and wait for its fruition in a completely detached way. Not only was Franklin able and willing to abandon the paternity of his ideas, but he also knew when the time was ripe for an idea and when the idea would have to wait.

How much Franklin could achieve by turning to the practical and mundane can be illustrated by looking at his inventions that improved daily life. The so-called Franklin stove allowed a more efficient use of wood. The lightning rod protected homes from a major source of fires. On a larger scale, Franklin and his *Junto* were instrumental in bringing about the Union Fire Company, the first of its kind. Sixteen years later, the mature entrepreneur formulated the revolutionary idea of the Union Fire Insurance Company, allowing the extension of the services of the Union Fire Company to a much larger part of the population.

It was not just Franklin's ideas that had a pervasive influence among the colonies. His tasks as postmaster for Philadelphia, and later as deputy postmaster general for the colonies, allowed him to cover a large territory. By age forty-two, Franklin had achieved economic independence. He was also the grand master of Pennsylvania Freemasons. In his own world, he had greatly contributed by holding a balance between the Quaker proprietors and the other forces of society, including the Freemasons. His presence was a key factor in defusing tensions between centrifugal tendencies, that is, tendencies that caused separation.

Promoting the Idea of America

In the next twenty years, Franklin's views expanded. His youthful wanderings in London played an important role in his education. In London, exposed to a rich cultural life, he came to see himself as a man of the British Empire. In his articles of belief at age twenty-two he had written: "that I may be loyal to my Prince and faithful to my country, careful for its good, valiant in its defense, and obedient to its Laws, abhorring Treason as much as Tyranny."

With good reason was Franklin called the "first American" before such an honor fell upon Washington's shoulders. The idea of America, of what made it different from any nation before that time, gradually matured in Franklin's mind. It is easy to underestimate Franklin's achievements because he lived in a world of ideas and personal relationships, rather than one of heroic deeds. He was a man of peace, whom some have called a "reluctant incendiary." Franklin's views evolved: he first thought the British Empire could evolve, but later he realized that America could blossom only away from the empire. From that point on, he was not at liberty to speak his mind candidly. He often had to veil his words or hide them under the subterfuge of a convenient pen name. That he could speak his mind at all was due to his reputation as scientist and philosopher and the popularity that preceded him wherever he went. We can retrace the steps that Franklin took in spirit and how they anticipated, as if in a blueprint, everything that later took shape in the world.

The first London exposure and the return to Philadelphia showed young Benjamin the disparity between the ideas of a cosmopolitan culture and the reality of empire on the economic level. From his vantage point in the world of business, he could not fail to notice that disparity. As early as 1747, the colonies' agent to London was advocating freedom of trade among the colonies. The first direct criticisms of British

44

imperialism and mercantilism appeared in 1751 in the *Observations Concerning the Increase of Mankind, Peopling of the Countries.* Here, although in a timid way, he was advising caution: "Britain should not too much restrain manufactures in her colonies." He is more pointed on the hidden costs of slavery: "The labor of slaves can never be so cheap here as the labor of working men in Britain."

Franklin emerged as a political figure on the American continental scene with the Treaty of Albany of 1754. That year was also a turning point for his thinking in economic matters. To Governor Shirley he outlined the burdens that the Americans carried from the prevailing practice of empire. He complained of the amount of indirect English taxes that the colonists had to pay, that is, the taxes incorporated into the English goods they imported. He perceived likewise the economic loss derived from enforced monopolistic purchases from and sales to England, given the preclusion of the colonies from other competitive markets. All of these impositions were, in fact, as he claimed, additional unspoken taxes paid to England.

But Franklin realized that the major obstacle to union between the colonies was, first and foremost, their own internal rivalries. Already in 1751 Franklin had written to James Parker, referring to the Iroquois: "It would be a very strange thing if Six Nations of Ignorant Savages should be capable of forming a Scheme for such an Union and be able to execute it in such a manner, as that it has subsisted Ages, and appears indissoluble, and yet a like Union should be impracticable for ten or a dozen colonies."[9]

By 1764, in what he could express privately to Peter Collinson, Franklin's views had evolved to a point hardly reconcilable with the prevailing English economic interests:

In time perhaps mankind may be wise enough to let trade take its own course, find its own proportions, etc. At present, most of the edicts of princes, placaerts, laws, and ordinances of kingdoms and states for that purpose prove political blunders. The advantages they produce, not being general to the commonwealth, but particular to private persons or bodies in the state who procured them, and at the expense of the rest of the people.

Yet for Franklin there was nothing economic that was not also a reflection of a human and moral dilemma. In the same letter, he wrote: "I think there is scarce anything you can do that may be hurtful to us but what will be as much or more so to you." What was true of human relations in general was all the more true of nations, no matter how it was expressed or disguised under codified economic relationships.

We have seen that Franklin was a man of the empire at first. However, his idea was an empire other than what British imperialism could tolerate. It was an empire of equal parts under one king. In it there could be no economic privileges sanctioned by political charter. The new politician clearly expressed this in 1754 at the Treaty of Albany. His *Plan for Settling Two Western Colonies* was a last-ditch effort to implement a larger empire of equals. Had his efforts been heeded, perhaps the American War of Independence could have been averted.

Over time Franklin came to realize how entrenched were the commercial and economic interests intimately intertwined with crown and Parliament. All of those he denounced cleverly or sarcastically in turn, often operating in disguise under the cover of a pen name. A variety of articles, essays, and pamphlets culminated in *An Edict of the King of Prussia* and *Rules by Which a Great Empire May Be Reduced to a Small One*. The second, in particular, written in 1773, can be considered a forerunner of the Declaration of Independence. In it were listed the grievances of the colonists against the mother country, in twenty points. Franklin advised prudence, but stood firm for American rights. Thus, it was only natural that he would assume a central role in the Continental Congress and the drafting of the Declaration of Independence. Behind the scenes, he had already walked in spirit the steps leading to independence.

Franklin's idea of America evolved from a larger universal idea of empire. His idea was almost a world federation before it turned by necessity into a specifically American federal system. The idea of the union of different parts, a sort of world brotherhood, came from Franklin's lifelong involvement with Freemasonry. After all, his spiritual brethren stretched to both sides of the ocean, as Franklin's later participation in French Freemasonry proved.

It was as a man of the world at large that Franklin promoted the idea of America in Europe. The American diplomat knew that if America was to become a new phenomenon in the world, it had to overcome deeply engrained cultural habits. While at home Washington was devising new ways to fight a battle of education, Franklin was fighting the diplomatic struggle that could win America's independence. He knew that he had to win over the French people. He also knew that he had to inaugurate a new era in international relations by trying to move away from political alliances and entanglements. He chose to focus on the arena of economic reciprocity—clearly stated mutual advantages—rather than the delicate balances of power at the mercy of a volatile political climate. In order to achieve this goal, he had to prevail over others, such as Arthur Lee and John Adams, who still operated within the old frame of mind.

A last aspect of Franklin's political life, worth mentioning here, concerns his relationships with the Native Americans. In 1736 Franklin had published his first account of a peace treaty with the Indians. During the next twenty-six years, Franklin published the accounts of another thirteen treaties. In the early 1750s, he became an Indian commissioner for Pennsylvania. He was surely familiar with the idea of federal union that the Iroquois chief Canassatego and other Indian chiefs advanced for the colonies. During the debate leading to the Treaty of 1744, Canassatego closed his speech with the following words: "Our wise forefathers established union and amity between the Five Nations. This has made us formidable. This has given us great weight and authority with our neighboring Nations. We are a powerful Confederacy; and by your observing the same methods our wise forefathers have taken, you will acquire much strength and power; therefore, whatever befalls you, do not fall out with one another."[10]

Franklin was defeated in his campaign for the Pennsylvania Assembly, probably for defending Indian rights during the episode of the Paxton massacre. After that episode, he wrote the impassioned text *A Narrative of the Late Massacres in Lancaster County of a Number of Indians, Friends of This Province, by Persons Unknown.*

New Consciousness and Grief

Franklin as a single individual had walked ahead of his people to wrest from the world of ideas a clear understanding of the existing reality, as well as of possible alternatives to it. He had to wait from the time of the Treaty of Albany in 1754 until a second chance presented itself in 1776. Once more a new idea awaited birth on the American continent. And once more, trials would be encountered along the way before the idea could be transformed into a new form. The suffering resulting from these trials would bring to birth a new consciousness and set the tone for the American dream.

The Declaration of Independence formed a watershed in the history of consciousness in North America. The colonists had acquired an understanding of the grievances that weighed on them; they could name the adversarial force and recognize it. This allowed them to overcome the differences among themselves. The core of the Declaration is in its first few sentences. In recognizing the divine origin of human beings, the Declaration acknowledged the higher self of the individual, which makes the individual worthy and able to govern itself. Since all are innately equal, they must have equal rights and be subjected to the same law. Implicitly the law is there to curb unrestrained expression of instincts and to protect society.

The Declaration of Independence was not the product of Jefferson's mind alone. Franklin and Adams had a part in revising it. The delegates from the colonies debated on it for three days and accepted it in varying degrees, until they finally made a show, at least, of unity. Franklin had a very important part in a different matter, a very decisive step. He was the one who signed the document declaring Washington to be commander of the Continental Army. Ironically, at the time of the signature, Washington was already in the field, successfully commanding the Continental Army. Here we see, already highlighted, the polarity between the two men. Franklin traveled through the world; Washington never left American soil. Although their life paths seldom crossed, there was a mutual, implicit recognition of one another.

During the low point of the war in 1780, Washington knew that his destiny lay with Franklin; he wrote to Franklin acknowledging that the only possible choices were either peace with Britain or financial support from France.[11] Seven years later, Franklin knew that proposing Washington as the president of the Constitutional Convention was a way to establish it on a firm ground of trust and consensus. And in 1793, at the inauguration of the presidency, Franklin offered a crab-tree walking stick to the "friend of mankind."

Once the message of independence had been spread, the commitment was going to be tested. The colonists, having recognized evil by its name, now had to face it. What Washington did was unique for a commander in chief in his time. He conducted a battle of education, which was education toward a new way of conceiving human relationships. It was this education that would supply the motivation to a mostly unprofessional army. This Washington accomplished on many levels. In the army he strove to dissolve personal attachments to separate colonies. The field lodges of Freemasonry served that purpose, mostly among the officers, although not exclusively. Freemasons, interestingly enough, ended up on both sides of the Revolution; they were among the Republicans as well as among the Loyalists. Nevertheless, a larger part of the Ancients sided with the Revolution. Freemasonry went on to play a larger role, as we will see later on. The universal appeal of the brotherhood attracted men from Europe, such as Von Steuben, De Kalb, Pulaski, Lafayette, and others, and compelled them to leave their countries and rally to the American cause. Washington requested the chaplains to call for prayers for the soldiers every day. On every account, the commander knew that he needed to receive help from the spiritual world.

Furthermore, Washington agreed to work in concert with a Continental Congress that was visibly weak and internally divided. This division caused painful delays to his military campaigns and imposed hardships on the army. His task was more difficult than what a high-ranking officer would have faced in a conventional army. He had to overcome the temptation to use his charisma to ease his situation. That would have hindered the very cause for which he was fighting. Working to educate, rather than to lead in an authoritarian way, also meant giving the benefit of the doubt and offering another chance to troublesome officers, as well as forgoing retaliation in order to promote unity.

A House Divided

These facts are generally well-known aspects of the Revolutionary War. Other factors, less well-known, played an important role in the resolution of the hostilities. The war was a painful civil war in more than one way. Britain's fight against the colonies often stood in conflict with the conscience of soldiers in the field. Freemasonry and the ideas of the social reformers reached across the battle lines. These were literally spiritual brothers who were at war with each other. When colonist de Kalb, mortally wounded, was found by Francis Rawdon, Cornwallis's second-in-command, Rawdon looked after de Kalb personally for three days. At his death, a Freemason ritual was performed. Accounts abound of troops on either side capturing Freemason regalia and returning it to the enemy. When the warrant of the Leicestershire Regiment was captured, Samuel Parsons returned it with these words: "When the ambition of monarchs, or the jarring interests of contending States, call forth their subjects to war, as Masons we are disarmed of that resentment which stimulates to undistinguished desolation; and however our political sentiments may impel us in the public dispute, we are still Brethren, and (our professional duty apart) ought to promote the happiness and advance the weal of each other."[12]

This loyalty certainly implied a delicate balancing act on both sides of the conflict. The split between military duty and spiritual allegiance lived in the higher echelons of the British Army. The obvious choice for leading the British Army was Lord Jeffrey Amherst, a Freemason. He declined twice, the second time after George III had appointed him commander in chief in America. There is ample evidence indicating that Sir William Howe and Lord Charles Cornwallis were also Masons. Twenty-nine of the thirty-one regiments that Howe led had warranted field lodges.[13] Howe's brother, Admiral Richard Howe, went so far in expressing his feelings as to declare the colonists the "most oppressed and distressed people on earth."[14] It seems small wonder, in light of these facts, that he squandered precious opportunities to press the Continental Army in its moments of debacle during the initial phase of the Revolution. Is it not surprising that Howe, after occupying Philadelphia, failed to exploit his superiority against the Continentals entrenched so close at hand at Valley Forge? Was Howe relieved, during the surrender at Yorktown, while his troops played the tune "The World Turned Upside Down"? We may never know for sure. However, from all the evidence, it is easy to surmise that ideas played a much larger role than is usually credited, in a place and time in which history looks primarily at military strategy.

The Issue of Slavery

Another painful wound was awakened by the Revolution: the issue of slavery. We can see how this confrontation lived in Washington. That Virginian, like many others, was the carrier of a guilt similar to the cannibalism of Hiawatha, that is, the guilt of a cultural condition inherited from birth. It was in the years of the war that Washington was first shocked to see free black men fighting in the New England army. Soon after, he was promoting desegregation for the African Americans in the Rhode Island contingents. One cannot help but wonder at the further impact of his meeting with Phyllis Wheatley, a former slave turned poet, who dedicated a poem to him. Washington reported being impressed by her presence. However, he could not fully address the problem of slavery during the war.

The way in which Washington tackled the problem of slavery showed that he could penetrate to its depths, which were in the economic realm that underlay the political form of the issue. By the end of his life, Washington had become a true pioneer in the field of agricultural practices. Having moved away from monoculture, he put his crops on a seven-year rotation plan. Plowland was systematically returned to grass, manure was treated with utmost care, and the soil was carefully fertilized. Every measure was applied to control erosion. All in all, we see a model tending toward the best of present-day diversified organic farming. Washington had truly attained a model of economic self-reliance and preservation of the environment. What Washington achieved spoke as an answer for the woes of the Southern economy. Tobacco or cotton monocultures were not only humanly degrading to the slaves; they were also ecologically devastating. Washington could have left no better testimonial than his farms. He followed up his agricultural testament by freeing his slaves. He was thereby showing that the human solution to the problem of slavery had to follow a shift to a different economic approach. His decision to free his slaves at the end of his life was a symbolic one amid the pervasive social forces that stood against it. Even in this instance, Washington pointed the way to the goal with his personal example.

The New Form

The war had been a necessary step for the dissolution of the old social structures. The same centrifugal forces (the divergent interests that separated the colonies) carried further would have made the nation vulnerable to foreign political and economic interests. A new political structure was necessary. When the need was finally felt, the Constitutional Convention gathered in Philadelphia. It served only an advisory function, and many doubted it could have any impact. The Declaration had inaugurated new cultural ground, but the convention had an eminently political and practical scope. It could not reach as high in a practical way as the Declaration had set out to do. Therefore compromise was needed.

The distances to be bridged were enormous: small states versus large states, proslavery delegates against abolitionists, moneyed and speculative interests versus demagogic tendencies, scholars and men of vision versus men pursuing strictly local political interest. There were no clearly drawn lines nor two defined sides; every delegate had his own mix of issues.

Primarily, what held the convention together was the fame and stature of many of its participants. Washington played a central role; two thirds of the delegates had links of destiny with him because of the roles he had played, not only in the Revolutionary War, but also in political office before that. His role as president of the Convention, however, condemned him to silence on the issues under discussion. He served as a facilitator, overseeing and guaranteeing the fairness of the process. His integrity standing beyond doubt, Washington seemed to be able to draw the best out of each person with whom he came in contact. Franklin was the oldest and could hardly be suspected of harboring partisan interests.

His wisdom played a great part, together with his humor and his ability to defuse tension.

We will look here only at the way the proceedings were conducted. In that process lay the secret of their success. The rules of listening had been so carefully laid out that it was not considered possible for any delegate to "occupy himself with foreign matter," interrupt, or in any way distract any speaker. To place things in perspective, some speakers held the floor for six hours. In the accounts of the four months of proceedings, there is hardly any mention of emotional outbursts. This is all the more remarkable for a convention conducted in the summer heat of Philadelphia.

The convention considered the matters at hand as if it were not faced by any practical limit of time. Issues were discussed for days and weeks. The delegates were truly meeting like their Iroquois counterparts, who were accustomed to discuss issues until unanimity could be reached. After such a process had arrived at a certain stage, mandate groups were chosen to draft propositions and plans. More important than the allowance for time was the allowance for reconsideration. Delegates were given the chance, and even encouraged, to reconsider their opinions. A decision already made and voted upon could still be reconsidered. Franklin's opinion on this process is worth quoting in full:

We are sent here to consult, not to contend with each other; declarations of a fixed opinion, and of determined resolution never to change it, neither enlighten nor convince us. Positiveness [rigid certainty] and warmth [heat] on one side, naturally beget their like on the other; (and tend to create and augment division in a great concern), wherein harmony and union are extremely necessary to give weight to our councils, and render them effectual in promoting and securing the common good.

In times of embarrassing silence, Franklin would invite the delegates to "speak their sentiments." Various delegates went from opposition to active support for the proposed constitution. Some of the major instigators of the idea, like Edmund Randolph, finally came out against it. Many endorsed it in spite of their objections because they saw in it the best possible outcome for such an effort. Others, like James McHenry, assented on the weight of the respect they held for the individualities assembled.

In the entire process, the best of Freemason practice and its code of conduct prevailed. The convention acted truly as a brotherhood. Opposition was more than simply tolerated; it was fully received and considered. This practice allowed opposition to play a role in the further development of events. Washington confided to Lafayette the feeling that a "Whitsun event" had occurred, where the result of the whole had become larger than what the sum of the participants could have achieved. "It appears to me, then, little short of a miracle that the delegates from so many different States, (which States you know are also different from each other) in their manners, circumstances, and prejudices, should unite in forming a system of national Government, so little liable to well-founded objections."

In the preamble to the Constitution, we see the famous phrase "We the People." The Constitution was submitted to the people, not to the state delegates. Franklin had previously expressed the need for that in the following words: "To get the bad customs of a country changed, and new ones, though better, introduced, it is necessary first to remove the prejudices of the people, enlighten their ignorance, and convince them that their interests will be promoted by the proposed changes; and this is not the work of one day."

Franklin's career reached its summit at the Constitutional Convention. He was the one suggesting Washington for president of the Convention, a major step in creating consensus. Franklin, as the eldest man, stood tall for his wisdom. It was not his ideas that won the delegates over (his ideas were often in the minority); rather, it was his faith in the future and his ability to reach fruitful compromises. In this light, his call to prayer acquires a role much greater than merely symbolic. So does his call to the delegates to rally to the newly proposed constitution in spite of its imperfections, real or perceived.

Parallels with the Iroquois League

The months following the convention saw the largest endeavors of political education on a national scale ever witnessed up to that point, and probably ever since. It was a political exercise of high quality, involving qualified orators and eager popular participation. The ratification process took ten months, longer than the convention itself. The process of education and the active opposition to the Constitution were sources of improvement to the final document. Provisions that had been fought against, or that had been thought to be self-evident, were then incorporated into the Bill of Rights. Many who had not favored the initial document could finally accept the amended version. Others, who remained opponents, felt that they still had the chance to contribute to further improvements. Once the result was achieved, many opponents felt they could join the majority. Overall, there were not strong dividing lines between losers and winners.

On September 18, 1793, the cornerstone of the United States Capitol building was dedicated by Washington, who was dressed in a Masonic apron. The silver plate placed upon the cornerstone indicated the thirteenth year of American independence, and the year 5793 of Masonry. Washington and his brethren, all in ritual vestments, covered the cornerstone with the symbols of corn, oil, and wine, Masonic representations of nourishment, refreshment, and joy. There could not have been a more explicit association of the ideals of the Republic with those held at the time by Freemasonry, and it was done by no less than the chief executive of the nation. Likewise, Washington's often-misunderstood effort as president to repudiate party politics was not an unrealistic utopian dream. It simply was the practice of the lodge and could not be attributed to naiveté in a man as shrewd and realistic as the president was.

In this presentation, we have emphasized only certain little-known parts, in order to make more visible the parallels between the Iroquois legend of *The White Roots of Peace* and the forming of the American federal system of government. Franklin and Washington played parallel roles to Deganawidah and Hiawatha. Hiawatha had been a cannibal; Washington was a slaveholder. This is not said to excuse either practice or condition, but to point to the cultural overarching element present across the centuries; this cultural element is something we are born into with no choice. Washington and Jefferson did not choose to acquire slaves;

they inherited that situation with their culture. British mercantilism created a context in which agriculture in the South would simply not have been economically sustainable had it not been for slavery.

The major steps of the process in the Iroquois legend repeated themselves: acceptance of a message and its proclamation, the trial and process of grief, overcoming and transformation of the evil that was fought against, and a new social form coming to birth. There seems to be an inner necessity to this dynamic in the way new ideas seek manifestation in social reality.

Chapter 3

From Squanto and Pocahontas:
The Dream of Brotherhood

Now is the time to lift our nation from the quicksands of racial injustice to the solid rock of brotherhood. Now is the time to make justice a reality for all of God's children.

—Martin Luther King Jr.

*T*he first two settlements on American ground, in Virginia and Massachusetts, have many more similarities than have been pointed out in historic literature. These similarities emerge when we look in particular at the kind of relationships established between Native Americans and colonists. What is less known is the fact that these two colonies are intimately united by intertwined biographies.

In my own biography, this theme captivated me through the Walt Disney movie *Squanto: A Warrior's Tale*. The movie was not quite an objective introduction to the theme, nor was it an accurate and historical rendering of facts. In fact, it was a lens that I had to discard because so much of it was inaccurate or sentimental. I remained determined to know more about this captivating biography, and in the attempt, to dislodge the Walt Disney perspective and other perspectives found in children's literature. I thought the facts would be easy to uncover, but that did not prove to be true.

First Americans: Links of Destiny

In the last fifty years, there has been a growing desire to pierce through the veil of the first Thanksgiving myth and to give this image some flesh-and-blood reality. This desire has resulted in a series of popular books, mostly for children, around the figure of the Native American Squanto. Among those we can mention are *Squanto and the First Thanksgiving* and *Squanto, Friend of the Pilgrims.*[1] Squanto's life is an astounding epic of unusual dimension for a Native American of the seventeenth century. Even though the authors fathom the interesting uniqueness of personal links and events in Squanto's biography, the results are moralistic and overly sentimental tales about the reconciliation of the races, an idealized rosy first Thanksgiving that simply does not correspond to reality. Still, there was much in the story itself that deepened my interest.

The ideal of the first Thanksgiving, with heart-to-heart understanding between natives and settlers, is something we may dream of, but we must admit we are still far from it. This was all the more true in the seventeenth century. Both the Virginia and Plymouth colonists came as Christians who regarded the natives as cruel, barbarous, and immoral. In addition, colonists with the rank of gentleman would rather remain idle than join hands to work with the commoners. The Puritans, or Separatists, regarded themselves as saints and everyone else as strangers. The natives themselves were at war with each other and used alliances with the newcomers to weaken their adversaries. Political and personal freedom was only an ideal, not a reality. Until the year 1618, the powers of the governor in the Virginia colony were practically powers of life and death. No less than some twenty offenses were punishable by death, and torture was also practiced. Among the listed crimes were such things as seeking shelter with the natives or accepting food from them, attempting to return to England, stealing food from the stores, or daring to criticize authority.[2]

When we steep ourselves in the mood of the time, the achievements of the three individuals we will consider acquire their true stature. Destiny forged links between the two colonies more strongly than is currently known. Individuals appeared at different times and places who were able to stand against the oppressive influences of environment, race, and culture. History seems to suspend its iron laws through the strength of one individual, or a few. This strength of individuality is what emerges in the story of the two colonies. Although many of the facts are already known to some extent, they will be at least briefly reviewed to highlight the degree of interconnection between the characters of this historic drama. We need look at only three individuals to reveal this web of special relationships: Captain John Smith, Squanto, and Pocahontas. The key events of their lives, relevant to this chapter, are summarized in the timeline below.

Time Line of Key Events in Jamestown and Plymouth Colonies

Squanto: c. between 1575 to 1580–1622

Captain John Smith: 1580–1631

Pocahontas: c. 1595–1617 (There are historical records for only 1607–1617.)

1601: Squanto was captured with four Abnaki natives on the coast of Maine by Captain George Weymouth. He was taken to England and lived with Ferdinando Gorges at Plymouth, England.

1607: Captain John Smith, a leader at Jamestown, met Pocahontas, who interceded with her father, Powhatan, for the life of Smith during the winter of 1607 to 1608.

1608: Smith released Indian prisoners on behalf of Pocahontas. She saved Smith again by telling him of a plot on his life.

1609: Smith left Jamestown for England, for treatment of a gunpowder wound. He contacted Ferdinando Gorges in Plymouth, England, and probably met Squanto. In Virginia, Pocahontas was told Smith was dead; she moved away from her father's tribe, joining a distant Native American tribe.

1613: Pocahontas was abducted by the English and taken away on a ship. She converted to Christianity, married John Rolfe, and had a son.

1614: Smith sailed back to America for a Maine expedition, accompanied by Squanto.

1615: In Maine, Smith's second-in-command, Dermer, vanished with one of Smith's boats. Smith was attacked by pirates. Squanto returned to his home village, only to be captured by Hunt (Smith's new second-in-command). Squanto was taken to Spain, where he was slave to a monk. Then he was sent (or escaped) to England; how and why are not known. He lived with John Slanie, president of the Newfoundland Company.

1616: Pocahontas left for England.

1617: Smith sailed to America with three ships (of thirty promised to him). Returning to Virginia, Pocahontas died en route in Gravesend, England.

1618: Squanto returned from England to Newfoundland on Slanie's ship; it is assumed he worked in commercial fishing.

1619: Smith had contact with Pilgrims; he wanted to lead them. They chose Standish instead, but they used Smith's maps.

Squanto sailed from Maine back to his home in Patuxent with Dermer. At this second homecoming, Squanto discovered his tribe was wiped out. He rescued Dermer's life from the natives, attempting to kill him.

1620: Squanto witnessed the arrival of the Pilgrims. Samoset introduced them to him.

1622: Squanto joined the Plymouth colony and converted to Christianity. He died of illness on a trading trip with Governor Bradford.

Captain John Smith (1580–1631)

At the end of his life, in London, an embittered lonely man, Captain John Smith made the claim that Plymouth and Jamestown were his two children.[3] Although a commoner by birth, Smith was one of the most well-traveled individuals of the times. He had fought as a soldier and mercenary, and first met glory in Eastern Europe and in Asia. This part of his biography is filled with gallant captures and escapes that are difficult to document from anything other than Smith's own words. Following these international escapades, he had a part in the founding of the Jamestown colony in 1607. In a way that was unusual at the time, he became the only commoner to be included in the council of the colony. However, he could not immediately assume his new task, because he had been charged with mutiny during the ocean journey. But when the written order for his leadership was unsealed, he was spared from the gallows.

Although the Virginia colony owed its initial survival to the cooperation between Smith and Pocahontas, the captain's stay in Jamestown was not to be long. He left after September 1609, needing to take care of a wound from an accidental explosion. In two years in Jamestown, he had proved his expertise in dealing with the Native Americans, although he often took advantage of their naïveté. He was practically the only leader who respected them and was able to refrain from senseless retaliations.

In 1609, in England, Smith contacted Ferdinando Gorges, (Englishman Ashton Phillips, who had taken the name Gorges and was appointed governor of the fort at Plymouth, England). Gorges became interested in colonizing the New World and was head of both the Plymouth Corporation and the North Virginia Company. Five years later, Smith sailed to America with an Indian named Squanto, of whom more will be said later,[4] Smith may have known Squanto during Squanto's captivity in England. At any rate, the American native was invaluable as an interpreter for trade dealings.

During the trip, Smith undertook on his own initiative to map the East Coast from Maine to Massachusetts. He was the one who gave their present names to Patuxet and Accomac (later Plymouth). The region that he explored he called New England, a name later confirmed by Prince Charles II.[5] Smith had other plans in mind. He hoped to establish a new colony, and Plymouth was the place of his choice. In the year 1615, he was ready to give shape to his plans, but his preparations had obviously been hasty. Captain Dermer, Smith's second-in-command, rapidly vanished with one of the boats. Smith's ship was damaged in a storm, and he had to return to Plymouth. He set out again, only to be attacked by pirates. The escapade made for an adventure that matched his reputation.

In 1617, another of his hurried plans saw him sailing for America with only three ships out of thirty that had been promised to him. For three months he had been ready to leave, but the weather stood against him and he hesitated. Not far away, Pocahontas, who had played an important part in his life, died at Gravesend, England, from a pulmonary disease in March of that year.

In 1620, if not already in 1619, Smith had made contact with the Pilgrims in order to lead them to America. They were reluctant to take on a man who could not stoop to any role but that of a leader. The famous Miles Standish was hired instead. Yet Smith still played a role. It was his maps that the Pilgrims took with them to the New World.[6] By another twist of fate, or possibly some hidden intention, the settlers landed in Plymouth rather than their initially intended destination at the mouth of the Hudson River. One cannot help but wonder if that happened by pure coincidence. After all, Plymouth had been indicated by Smith as a good site for colonization.[7] Thus they reached the land to which Squanto had returned (although briefly) less than a year before.

Smith's life shows in a compelling way the network of relationships involved in the founding of the first two colonies. He is the tragic embodiment of a life failing to bring about its intended fruition, whether at Jamestown or Plymouth. The captain formed personal relationships with the two individuals whose lives shine as radiant symbols in the evolution of the two colonies: Squanto and Pocahontas.

Squanto

For a time it was believed that there were two individuals with the name of Squanto (sometimes written Squantum or Tisquantum).[8] This seemed the best way to explain how his name kept reappearing, seeming to move from one side of the Atlantic Ocean to the other. It has taken some time for historical research to put the pieces together and figure out that the name belongs to just one individual.

Squanto belonged to the Patuxet, an Algonquian tribe of Massachusetts, residing in the area of present-day Plymouth. He was born sometime between 1575 and 1580. His name first appears in the records of the expedition of Captain George Weymouth. Squanto had been captured with four others, Abnakis from the coast of Maine. This leads some to believe that he may have been on a journey to the Maine Algonquian tribe. In England, he lived with Sir Ferdinando Gorges of the Plymouth Company. Gorges described Squanto in his three-volume memoir.

Squanto remained in England for nine years before he had the opportunity to return home with an expedition led by Captain Smith. It was a return for both of them. At the end of the journey, Squanto was released at Cape Cod, and from there made it back to his tribe in Patuxet.

Thanks in large part to Smith's tolerant views, a conciliatory mood between the colonists and the native Indians had been established. In gratitude, the Patuxet held a celebration. Captain Hunt, Smith's second-in-command, took advantage of the Patuxets' relaxed attention to invite twenty-four of them aboard his ship. Once there, he made them captives and took them to Spain to sell them as slaves.

Squanto gained the relatively privileged position of being a slave to a monk. How Squanto made it back to England four years later has not been documented. He found refuge there with a John Slanie, who was the treasurer and later the president of the Newfoundland Company (also called the Bristol Company).[9] Aboard one of Slanie's ships, Squanto made it back to the American continent in 1618, but only to Newfoundland. He was probably working for the fishing industry. The next year, he sailed back home with Captain Thomas Dermer, who worked for the Plymouth Company.

This second homecoming was the harshest trial for Squanto. He discovered that his tribe had been entirely wiped out, most likely by an outburst of chicken pox or measles. The years of exile and the loss of all his bloodline were the fruits of his contact with the white race. Soon after his return, the familiar pattern of deceptions and reprisals was to play yet another role in Squanto's life. This time it was to come through Captain Dermer, who had worked with Smith. After a senseless massacre committed by an English trader, the natives of the Wampanoag Confederation intended to retaliate by killing Dermer, who was there for trade. Squanto saved his life.

Squanto was now without a people and he had raised the suspicion of the neighboring tribes for his defense of a white man, so he returned with Dermer to Plymouth, where he witnessed the arrival of the Pilgrims. He was introduced to them two months later by Samoset, a sachem of the Abnaki of Maine, with whom Squanto had most likely been acquainted prior to his first abduction. There in Plymouth, he joined the settlement permanently. Squanto's vital role in the colony has been abundantly acknowledged. He helped the settlers to grow crops and to fish for their sustenance. As an interpreter, he helped to bring about the successful peace treaty that the Pilgrims drafted and eventually signed with the natives. More importantly, he helped to assure trade with the neighboring tribes.

Squanto's last years were marred by a climate of suspicion and distrust. Massasoit, the Wampanoag sachem, had sent an ambassador to the Pilgrims in the person of Hobomok. Rivalry developed between the two Indians and the Pilgrims took sides, partly in order to obtain major gains for themselves. Squanto attempted to strengthen his position by gaining power among the Wampanoag. To that end, he used the natives' superstitious fears of English weapons and diseases and their belief that he had English support. Once this intrigue was discovered, only the Pilgrims could save Squanto from Massasoit's death decree. This they did in memory of all the help they had received from him. He died of an illness in 1622, while on a trading expedition with Governor Bradford. It appears that he converted to the Pilgrims' faith before his death.

Squanto carried further the process of rising above racial blood ties, which Smith had initiated with Pocahontas. His destiny placed him in an even more dramatic position. He was well on the way to forming a bridge between the two cultures. Only later did he resort to cunning, succumbing to the prevailing atmosphere of distrust and deception.

Among the lesser participants of the founding drama of America, we have heard Dermer's name appear twice, first in relation to Smith, then associated with Squanto. His life course was shaped by the forces at play, although he seemed to stand at the mercy of external factors that played alternatively in his favor and against him. Dermer was supposed to be part of the intended Plymouth colony in 1615. When he returned there in 1619, Squanto saved him from Massasoit's vengeance. In the same year, he traveled to Martha's Vineyard in order to trade. There he met with Epanow, sachem of the natives, who at one point had also been a captive of the English. Epanow, afraid that Dermer might be there to capture him, killed all his party and left him with wounds that probably caused his death a year later in Virginia.

Pocahontas

In her lifetime she was called Pocahontas; her secret family name was Matoaka; finally, she became Lady Rebecca.[10] Pocahontas was in fact a nickname by which she was known outside of the tribe. It meant "playful, mischievous, frolicsome." Her real name, Matoaka, was a secret name known only by the closest members of her clan, but not used in everyday life.

A vast number of books have been written on her account over the last century and a half, and the flow has not dried up. The historical records cover only the last ten years of her life, from 1607 to 1617, and she even disappears for four of these years (1609 to 1613). That such a fleeting historical presence should cause her to become a legend is enough to prove the depth of her impact on the American (and European) mind.

In her short life, the Powhatan princess gives proof of independence of mind, together with sound judgment, strength to carry out her resolves, compassion, and adaptability. Being the favorite daughter of Powhatan, the chief of an Indian confederacy, gave her a status and respect with natives and Englishmen alike that neither Squanto nor Smith could attain.

In the well-known first reported episodes of her life, she was the one who became acquainted with Captain Smith and taught him the rudiments of her Algonquian language. In the winter of 1607–08, when Smith was captured by Powhatan, Pocahontas interceded for his life. Whether it was a real rescue or a ritualized mock execution, the ordeal strengthened Smith's ties with the confederacy.

The colonists were plagued by continuously fluctuating relationships with the natives, as well as by their own inertia and bitter rivalries. During the first two winters, it was Pocahontas who assured the survival of the settlers by allowing them access to food supplies. She seemed to act independently of her father already; he was still undecided about what policy to follow with the foreigners. Pocahontas also had a restraining effect on Smith; on her behalf, he released Indian prisoners in June 1608.

Events accelerated dramatically at the end of 1608. Powhatan banned trade with the colonists and moved far from them to Werowocomoco, his capital. Powhatan actually planned to kill Smith, who came on a trading mission. It was Pocahontas who saved him by unveiling her father's intentions; this showed that she was distancing herself further from Powhatan's policies. Displaying a complete lack of sensitivity, Smith wanted to reward her with trinkets.

Smith was later relieved of his power and ended up accidentally wounded in an attempt to form a separate colony. That is when he left the colony and Pocahontas was told that he had died. His departure left the diplomat Pocahontas without any intermediary. A cycle of senseless cruelty from the colonists and retaliations from Powhatan set in. In 1609, Powhatan ordered the massacre of sixty settlers.

Pocahontas moved away, to the farthest reaches of the confederacy, to the Patawomekes, a tribe that enjoyed a degree of autonomy from Powhatan. It was a sacrifice on her part. She relinquished her status of privilege. Probably because of her influence, the Patawomekes were the only ones who kept trading with the whites. Pocahontas also had a hand in saving Henry Spelman, a hostage who had escaped from Powhatan and was threatened with death from his ex-captives.

It is in the least expected way that Pocahontas played the role of mediator she seemed to be yearning for. In 1613 she was abducted by the colonists. This episode was followed by her conversion to Christianity and her marriage to John Rolfe, a recently arrived settler. Pocahontas had to sacrifice the freedom of her ways in order to adapt to a rigid code of ethics. Yet she did it willingly. From this simple step emerged what was called the peace of Pocahontas; it was even dubbed a honeymoon between the races. Pocahontas brought her relatives and servants to live with her, inaugurating a level of cohabitation between the races unknown until that time. In the wake of these events, greater tolerance prevailed between colonists and natives.

In the spring of 1616, Pocahontas went to England. Behind the stated purpose of promoting a Christian school for English and native children was the more substantial promotional aspect that the Virginia

Company needed. At the time, it was still struggling to remain afloat and encourage new colonists. Pocahontas suffered from various challenges. It was in England that Pocahontas met again with John Smith, whom she had believed dead. We can only surmise the impact of the encounter and whether this was another contributing factor, in addition to the culture shock and the poor sanitation in London, that led her to contract what seems to have been a respiratory disease. She died in March 1617.

Colonialism: Blotting Out Brotherhood

In the drama of the foundation of the new nation, a host of actors play important roles. By looking at three of them, whose lives we have just examined, we can touch upon most of the central issues and uncover significant relationships. The lives of the three main individuals highlight how their choices led to different outcomes. We can marvel at how the lives of these individuals kept intersecting in a way that has very little to do with mathematical probability or random chance. It might seem to be pure speculation to wonder at the effects of courageous individual decisions or to envision scenarios that did not occur. This is not an idle exercise, however. Individual destiny is not an inescapable, preset path. It leaves open many choices and often offers individuals more than one opportunity to achieve certain goals.

In the society of the seventeenth century, Smith's natural capacities, standing, and authority were of no avail against social prejudices. His relentless assertiveness and complete lack of tact were his downfall. Those qualities also played against him in the minds of the Pilgrims; Miles Standish was chosen as their leader instead.

The vacuum created by Smith's absence from Jamestown required all the more energy and willingness on the part of Pocahontas. It remains pure speculation to contemplate what Plymouth could have been with the help of both Smith and Squanto, who already knew each other. Ironically, it was in Miles Standish that Squanto found a resolute adversary. The Native American faced a different temptation than Smith did. Not having the charisma and sheer bravado of the captain, Squanto resorted to cunning and deceit in order to circumvent the distrust of both natives and settlers.

Pocahontas: Rising above Race

In Pocahontas, a process was brought to completion. She had the strengths of both Smith and Squanto. In addition, she could stand above the warring parties with firmness and compassion. By her unwillingness to accommodate, compromise, or seek an outlet for personal ambition, she managed to fulfill what seems to have been her life task. To accomplish this task, she willingly paid the price imposed by the deceit of the colonists and the Virginia Company. Although there are no documents that prove this, looking at the whole tenor of her life and commitments, and her demeanor, one can conclude that there seems to be nothing artificial in Pocahontas's acceptance of Christianity. It came to her through Alexander Whitaker, a man who had left a life of ease to come to Virginia and who showed complete tolerance toward the natives.[11] Through him, John Rolfe was able to overcome his pangs of consciousness at the idea of marrying a "savage" woman.

The contradictory future of the colony was fittingly represented by the ambivalent image of John Rolfe. His devotion and earnestness seem genuine. Through him came both the peace of Pocahontas and the rescue of the Virginia Company's financial interests. It was Rolfe who successfully introduced the tobacco culture into the new colony, assuring it an economic outlet. Rolfe could not see the full implication of his experiments, other than the fact that they assured him a place in society well beyond his humble origins. He witnessed and recorded the arrival of the first cargo of African slaves brought by a Dutch boat in 1619 without registering the full impact of this precedent.

Through Pocahontas's devoted life, history momentarily escaped the unavoidable dynamic that the stronger political and economic forces of the moment brought to the surface. A sort of island in space and time was created by the commitment of an individual fully living on the strength of her moral intuitions, even at the cost of repeated sacrifice.

In Pocahontas, the ideal of brotherhood was strongly rooted. Although she stood within the forces of race, religion, and culture, as did her contemporaries, the vigor of her individuality rose above them. Her moral feelings and principled positions would surely puzzle one who believes only in racial, social, or environmental determinism.

Destiny is a mysterious concept for some, an intuited reality for others. The individual can either accept destiny passively, with a feeling of fatalism, or blindly rebel against it. There is also a third, intermediate possibility. We can call it active acceptance, but it could also be called active questioning. Active acceptance is an attitude that questions the given social and environmental conditions of the times. It challenges them with a constructive attitude that achieves a balance between the opposite poles of pure rebellion and strict conformity. It stems from the realization that our life has a set of constraints from which we can free ourselves and another set of constraints that we must learn to accept.

An implicit element of active acceptance is the capacity to forgive. In order to forgive, the individual must fully know the pain of the offense that has been inflicted upon him or her. He or she must build the strength and desire to be able to give back to the world as much as has been taken away through the offending deed.

The strength of individuality, which actively accepts her life challenges and offers forgiveness, is recognizable in Pocahontas. Pocahontas's resolve for forgiveness brought about the ensuing years of peace. She had formed a solid connection with the colonists via Captain Smith and provided for their survival, even facing her father's disapproval in doing so. She had forgiven Smith's behavior when she resolved to marry Rolfe. Throughout her life, she strove to bring about the recognition of the universal spiritual element that unites communities beyond race, culture, or religion. In this light, her conversion experience is secondary. There is no marked difference between her behavior before or after it.

Seen without the elements of acceptance and forgiveness, Pocahontas's life becomes a legend. Her behavior escapes a purely deterministic paradigm. Of all the actors on the scene of the founding of the colonies, she was the least predictable because she was the most determined from within. It is in the ideal of brotherhood that Pocahontas became the first American heroine, as she has been fittingly named.

Individuals and Corporations

The future of America lay encapsulated in the contrast between Pocahontas and the Virginia Company. The corporation ruled its territory like a business or a production unit. It was a symbol of the monopolies that exploited the colonies for the mother country. Monopolies rested on the alliance between the political system and the economy. Merchants would benefit from the exclusion of all competition; politicians would benefit from the company's fortunes. The Virginia Company would naturally have to be supported by the might of England's navy. The fate of an economic-financial pursuit thus came to be confused with, and assimilated into, the interests of the English people at large.

In America the Virginia Company promoted the development of monoculture. The fate of the southern colonies, as was clear from a quick examination of mercantilism, was a destiny of debt. The planters could not support themselves free of debt, even having access to the free labor of slaves. Slavery itself embodies the ultimate state of debt. The slave's life is not his to decide upon. He owes it to somebody else. The slaves' individualities were blotted out in order to make of them mere mechanisms in a production unit.

It is not easy to see, at first, that Pocahontas was a polar opposite to this first image. The Indian princess ended her life at the hand of the greed of the Virginia Company that used her as a promotional tool. Before that, Pocahontas's generosity and open-mindedness unlocked new possibilities for others. Being the daughter of a king allowed her to extend help to Captain Smith. When she lost the support of both Smith and her father, she was still trading with the English through the Patawomekes and keeping a door open for peaceful collaboration. Even her abduction opened new possibilities through her ensuing marriage. Through her agency, other individuals were given back the ground wherein their human potential could fully develop. Pocahontas took upon herself acceptance accompanied by willed self-sacrifice. This was the sacrifice of personal ambition, desire for power over others, and other life-negating natural human urges. Through this sacrifice, she did not renounce her own quest for happiness. It appears that she could find happiness, as well as providing the ground for other people's happiness.

To the sacrifice imposed on others by the Virginia Company, Pocahontas offered the complement of healthy self-sacrifice that opens new, creative paths in the social body. This image aptly summarizes the contrast between world visions that stood visible at the drama of America's founding.

For an even partial defeat of the economic policies of British imperialism, new impulses needed to gain strength. Washington and Franklin arrived at the culmination of a dynamic begun by the lesser-known and unaccounted heroes like Squanto and Pocahontas. The two founding fathers could play a larger role in history precisely because the ground had already been richly prepared.

Going even further, we could examine certain eighteenth- and nineteenth-century political and spiritual phenomena in this light. For example, was it mere chance that Philadelphia acted as the midwife to a process of innovation culminating in the new form of government? Was not Philadelphia already the center of what was called the Holy Experiment, a haven for persecuted people and ideas? There, the relationships between colonists and Native Americans, although not perfect, had at least another tenor; wars were avoided. Did not such cultural ferment attract the brilliant mind of Franklin and allow the development of countless of his ideas? Did not it allow Franklin to understand and appreciate the ideas of the Iroquois? In between these stages, we could mention the role played by the Moravian missionaries in Pennsylvania and the role played by Conrad Weiser (a young man who had been raised by the Iroquois) as emissary of the colony to the Native Americans. These small turning points, like the peace of Pocahontas, may be swallowed by the course of history and seemingly amount to little, but the social healing created by them is real and enduring. They provide the foundations for later fundamental changes.

What remained of the efforts of individuals like Pocahontas and Squanto did not die. It found another shape in a Thanksgiving holiday that the American soul longed for. We will return to this in chapter 4.

Chapter 4

What Can We Save from the Past?

Fellow citizens, the signers of the Declaration of Independence were brave men. They were great men too—great enough to give fame to a great age. It does not often happen to a nation to raise, at one time, such a number of truly great men.

—Frederick Douglass

*T*he myths, legends, and history surveyed in chapters 1 through 3 have been enshrined in the national consciousness. George Washington has been honored on Washington's Birthday; it was the first holiday to celebrate an American individual. (It was later expanded to include Lincoln on Presidents' Day.) The events and impulses that led to the Declaration of Independence and Constitutional Convention find their echoes in the Fourth of July celebrations. Finally, the figures of Squanto and Pocahontas acquire a particular significance in relation to Thanksgiving.

The Promise of a New Culture

Washington and Franklin set the course for the New World in contrast to anything that had held true in the social reality of the Old World. To the idea that all men were created equal followed the momentous wager of a form of government determined by the people and intended for the people. The revolution would not have been possible without the process of education that General Washington and Congress had to undergo in their mutual relationships. The results of the Constitutional Convention would not have become reality without a process of education of the whole nation, leading to the ratification of the constitution.

No national holiday recognizes the nation's indebtedness to Benjamin Franklin. The previous chapters have outlined the uniqueness of this individual in relation to the culture of the eighteenth century and shown the central role he played in educating the country to its world task. His stature calls for an acknowledgment that should ultimately take the form of a celebration in the calendar of the year. Meanwhile, similar holidays have been dedicated to the memory of Washington and Lincoln.

Washington's Birthday and Presidents' Day

Congress first established a federal holiday honoring George Washington in 1879. Washington's Birthday was first the interest of the Capitol alone, but by 1885, it included all federal offices. This first holiday by which America honored one of its citizens was at first regularly held on February 22, the date of Washington's birthday. In 1971 it was moved to the third Monday in February.

In recognition of what was already being celebrated in a dozen states, there was an attempt to change the name to Presidents' Day to honor at the same time Washington and Lincoln (whose birthday was February 12). This explains why the date chosen in 1971 falls between the two dates. In some places, the holiday had been renamed Presidents' Day or even Washington and Lincoln Day. Although the proposal was not accepted at the time, we have now moved in that direction, and we cannot but help see the thread between the two presidents, as it had been pointed out to Washington in the second tableau of his vision at Valley Forge, the part of the vision that points to a civil war and to the threat associated with Africa.

In bringing together remembrance of Washington and Lincoln, the American soul showed a yearning for completion. What Washington accomplished for his century, Lincoln moved forward in the following century. No president left as powerful a stamp on American history as Washington, our first president. No president was as deeply imbued with spiritual and moral forces as was Lincoln, our sixteenth president. Washington was the first famous slave-owner to free his slaves. His

74

insight about the root cause of slavery and his desire to see this social ill uprooted found a continuation in Lincoln.

The moral impulse toward freedom that propelled Lincoln in the nineteenth century needed a continuation in the twentieth, and that is what Martin Luther King Jr. brought into further manifestation. Not surprisingly, another personal holiday has been created for him. This is a continuation of what finds expression in America as the land of the free. Chapter 5 explores King's life and influence on our society.

The Call for Equality: A Contrast between Two Revolutions

The striving behind the American Revolution metamorphosed into the powerful longing for new political forms, for the overcoming of monarchy and colonialism, and for the realization of a government of, by and for the people. The nature and unique achievement of the American Revolution can best be appreciated when seen in contrast to its close counterpart in France, which took place in 1789, only two years after the American Constitutional Convention. Independence Day, July 4 in America, and Bastille Day, July 14 in France—these are the two events, close in time and in the calendar, that marked the beginning of the respective revolutions.

The long pent-up aspirations of the people on both sides of the Atlantic found their fullest expression in the heat of summer. The French Revolution started on July 14, 1789, with an event markedly different from the quiet signing of the Declaration of Independence. The storming of the Bastille was an insurrection reflecting the utter despair of the French people. To them, the hated Bastille fortress symbolized tyranny and oppression. This act of revolt was followed by violence, and later by the infamous Reign of Terror. All of it was reflected in the philosophy of the Declaration of the Rights of Man and Citizen of August 27, 1789. In it a divine principle is mentioned only once. In later documents, the divine is never mentioned again. The preamble states that the document is a "solemn declaration of the natural, inalienable rights of man." The French constitution of 1791 stated: "The law no longer recognizes religious vows or any obligation contrary to natural rights of the Constitution." The third constitution of Robespierre said in article 9: "Every citizen owes his services to the Motherland, and to the maintenance of liberty, equality, and property, whenever the law summons him to defend them." Beginning from the first document and more so with the succeeding ones, the human being was divorced from all connection to the spirit, subordinated to the state, and elevated at most to the rank of citizen. Napoleon's dictatorship was the necessary outcome of a spiraling cycle of violence, as German Romantic poet Friedrich Schiller had predicted. Napoleon's self-crowning stands in stark contrast to Washington's refusal of the crown.

Freemasonry had advanced powerful ideas also in France. Its teachings inspired the call to liberty, equality, and fraternity. Nevertheless, the Freemason brotherhood in France had lost its vigor, the vital link with the spiritual inspiration capable of bringing about social changes. Freemasonry's internal weaknesses, as well as the opposing forces of church and state, brought about a completely different outcome. Anticlericalism (although perfectly understandable in light of the place and role of the French Catholic Church) became almost a rage against every spiritual idea. By the time of Napoleon, nationalism and the cult of personality had practically obliterated the initial striving for renewal.

In America, through the consciousness infused into the Declaration of Independence and all the subsequent steps leading to the ratification of the Constitution, moral forces were consciously mastered and put into serving the social compact. Emotionalism and gratuitous outbursts of violence had, to a great degree, been carefully avoided. Spiritual forces had truly brought about a very tangible renewal of society.

Although the American Revolution seems the more sober of the two revolutions, it is precisely that soberness wherein lies the opportunity for equality. The French enraptured love of total equality, closely connected with utopian ideology, ultimately led to extremism and new forms of tyranny. Violence can only return us to conditions that bring inequality and domination.

The Dream of Equality and the Reality

George Washington and Benjamin Franklin, together with other great figures of their time, brought the dream of equality that is enshrined in the Declaration of Independence. With hindsight, we could fault them, and others, for what the time was not yet ready to achieve. The Constitution was an imperfect work, demanding the vigilance of all future generations. Within it already lay the seeds of future conflicts that would be struggles for its furtherance and improvement. The matter of equality between the white and the black races could not have been resolved in the eighteenth century within a united nation. The question of women's rights had not been present for even a moment.

On their own, Franklin and Washington had already envisioned and accomplished much that was ahead of their time. In particular, Washington had understood the economic roots of slavery and pointed the way to the overcoming of that ill. Two great struggles would have to follow in the name of equality for all human beings, which the Declaration of Independence upheld: the first was the struggle for African-American equality that Lincoln furthered, and the second was that of women. In these strivings was renewed the Declaration of Independence call that "all men [human beings] are created equal." Chapter 6 recounts the history of the struggle for women's rights in the United States.

The parallels between the American and the French Revolutions are more crucial than they appear at first sight. The ideals of liberty, equality, and fraternity, which were enshrined in the clarion call of the French Revolution, were drowned in the din of violence. The extreme demand that the state guarantee absolute equality wiped out the possibility for freedom and brotherhood. Although this "sacred three" was never taken up as consciously in America, it was present in the American dream. These three ideals are woven into what seems to be a universal human yearning. We have found them in the first part of this book, and they continue to be an integral part of present aspirations and of visions of the future.

The Yearning for Brotherhood

Brotherhood finds its own arena in the life of the economy and survives in the ideal of America as the land of opportunity for all. This striving can be examined in the colonies and in the way it later emerged in the national consciousness.

The two earliest colonies, Plymouth and Jamestown, although starkly different, have a similarity from an economic perspective. Both the South Virginia (London) and North Virginia (Plymouth) companies, responsible for the establishment of the two colonies, were issued charters in the spring of 1606. They were both responsible to the Royal Council of Virginia and were governed by similar commercial and financial interests. The centralized form of government that derived from the companies' instructions preserved little of the cherished freedoms of the Englishmen.[1]

As early as 1676 in Virginia, all Indian prisoners of war were judged to be slaves for life under a ruling of law.[2] However, the measure proved unsuccessful in subjugating the natives' will. The poor were brought from Europe to work in the colonies as indentured servants; they made up the majority of the Virginia labor force. True, the indenture would last for no longer than seven or eight years, and under those terms, labor paid for the sea voyage and for food and lodging. This system offered relief to individuals and families eager to escape economic or political oppression in Europe. However, the indentured individual had little protection or recourse of law if he served under an abusive master. In addition to indentured servitude, there was enforced servitude, which was the lot of criminals, prisoners of war, and vagrants of the English crown. Their free labor offered them an alternative to jail time.

The ultimate cruelty of the English monopolistic economy and colonialism was demonstrated in the fate of African slaves. A 1669 ruling specifically enforced that "if any slave resist his master (or other by his master's order correcting him) and by the extremity of the correction should chance to die, that his death shall not be accompted ffelony [sic]."[3] The same was true in the case of runaways. In fact, no form of cruelty was excluded, whether imprisonment, torture, branding, or separation from close family members. No matter how extreme the measures, escaping to freedom still proved too tempting to slaves and to those indentured servants who could not alter their lot through the law.

This situation had deep roots in the prevailing economic system. Once it was politically emancipated, the United States still competed with English world economic power in the global market of the time. The economic conditions following American independence painfully reminded the new country that world powers still imposed world economic conditions. Nowhere was this more true than in the agrarian American South.

Thanksgiving Holiday

The longing for true solidarity between the races was nevertheless present in the American soul, and it finds a fitting expression in the Thanksgiving holiday, a holiday that saw its birth with the end of slavery and the Civil War. In Thanksgiving, the greatly cherished figures of Pocahontas and Squanto find their place and meaning, representing the yearning for the opposite of what the British Empire embodied. Pocahontas and Squanto represented another significant expression of the American dream.

Thanksgiving is the holiday of family intimacy, a celebration of home and hearth. In this sense, it contrasts strongly with the national Fourth of July. Thanksgiving calls on the warmth of relationships, rather than the light of great ideals. It is the celebration of the return to our origins: familial, cultural, and religious. Such a simple, unpretentious celebration had to struggle longer than the other celebrations before gaining acceptance as a national holiday.

The date of the first Thanksgiving is contested. New England folklore places it first in the autumn of 1621, in Plymouth, Massachusetts. Virginians claim an earlier one on April 29, 1607, the first celebration officially held on Virginian soil by the Jamestown colony. Regardless of the claims, Thanksgiving is characteristically a New England festival. It evolved primarily in the towns of the Plymouth colony and the Connecticut River. In 1639 it was first proclaimed a state holiday in Connecticut. By 1649 it had become a regular celebration there and was held every year thereafter in autumn. The celebrations included four hours of morning religious services and a home meal, followed by another two hours of service. By the beginning of the 1700s, the celebration had spread to Massachusetts and New Hampshire, and the feast became as important as the morning religious service.

During the American Revolution, Thanksgiving gradually became politicized. The first national Thanksgiving, on December 18, 1777, honored Arnold's and Gates's victory at Saratoga. In 1789 President Washington declared a Thanksgiving Day for the blessing of the new form of government. He proclaimed only one other, in 1795. On this occasion he was very careful to include "all religious denominations ... and all persons." There was no reference to Christianity in his message. From this point onward, the holiday had to achieve Washington's goal and include any religious or political outlook.

Thanksgiving celebrates our ordinary ancestors. Likewise, it was a seemingly ordinary woman who spread the conviction that the festival should become a national holiday. Native to New Hampshire in 1788, Sarah Josepha Hale became a widow with five children in her charge. She decided to support her family with her literary gifts and wrote a rather controversial book, which focused on the contrasts between the North and the South. It was called *Northwood, or Life North and South*. On the strength of her success, she accepted a job as editor of *Ladies' Magazine*, one of the first women's magazines. Through this publication and her undeterred canvassing, she campaigned for a national Thanksgiving beginning in 1846. Not surprisingly, it was Lincoln who heeded her call.

A major fault line appeared at the time of the Civil War. The religious denominations split along North-South and proslavery versus anti-slavery lines. The holiday was called twice by Lincoln: first in 1863, then the following year, when it became a national holiday. Official proclamations notwithstanding, many of the Southern states resented the adoption of a festival instated by Lincoln, and associated with the Union victory. In the South, it was often either skipped or used to celebrate victories for white supremacy rule. In addition, because Thanksgiving had been initially a Protestant holiday, Catholics viewed it with suspicion. It was only in 1884 that it was adopted by the Plenary Council of Catholic Bishops in Baltimore. Consequently, Thanksgiving began to be celebrated with united services of an interdenominational character. All things considered, it took more than two centuries for Thanksgiving to evolve into a national holiday. Even after that, the festival could not quite become a national reality until all factional wounds were healed to a degree.

Thanksgiving has been the holiday of assimilation. Innumerable new immigrants to the land have been able to adapt to the minimal requirements that the celebration places on culture or religion: that we are all children of God, and brethren regardless of the color of our skin or the nature of our personal beliefs. This is the ever-present sign of the dream of a land of many lands and a land of opportunity that has found its expression in America.

Under the Shadow of the American Dream

Deganawidah, Tamanend, Washington, Franklin, and Lincoln (or rather, the roles that they played as spiritual/moral leaders) were powerful announcements of the freedom that can be experienced by every individual through the infusion of new values into the fabric of culture. Freedom is the value that can derive only from the vibrant life of an independent civil society. The presence of a strong cultural impulse is what made the American Revolution essentially different from the French.

We have given some examples of the number and variety of civic associations that existed at the inception of the United States. The colonies, even while politically dominated by England, had developed a considerable network of cultural institutions, as we saw in Franklin's Philadelphia; likewise, religion had taken a great variety of expressions. States like Pennsylvania were devoted to a whole new experiment and predicate for society. French culture, in contrast, had still been subjugated by both the tyranny of the king and the dogma of the church, which overwhelmed and stifled most independent cultural initiatives. The words *America, land of the free* may have become a cliché in the present, but they expressed some truth, at least in times past.

The federal government that emerged from the Declaration of Independence and the Constitutional Convention made a growing equality possible for the first time in world history. The unique sets of checks and balances of executive, legislative, and judiciary were designed to this effect. In the vision of the American dream, all individuals, no matter what their role, may be called by their first names because "all men are created equal." Whether this is the case today is a legitimate question; still, the yearning continues to survive.

A major part of the American dream lives in the expression *America, land of opportunity.* America was seen in the past as the nation in which all immigrants could start their lives anew with equal opportunities. And countless immigrants have indeed thrived and been assimilated by American culture, finding here what they could not reach in their own country. What was once true, however, has become a myth, a cliché of the past. The current reality speaks otherwise. Here are some numbers. In 2004/2005 (according to census data), the top 20 percent of the US population owned 84.4 percent of the national wealth; the bottom 20 percent had no worth to speak of, or rather, debts to pay off.[4]

The land that was born as a counter to colonialism has now become the center of world empire. From its center ray out into the world the realities of worldwide political, economic, and financial exploitation and subjugation of cultures and countries around the globe. No other country has played such a major part in the depletion of the world's resources, degradation of the environment, and alteration of world climate. Still, in the United States the yearning for world solidarity finds one of its most powerful expressions. And the impulse that gave birth to Thanksgiving has returned in Earth Day, the promising new national and global holiday that chapter 7 describes.

Part IS:
Stories: Resisting
the Nightmare

The U. S. Constitution doesn't guarantee happiness, only the pursuit of it. You have to catch up with it yourself.

—Benjamin Franklin

Chapter 5

Martin Luther King Jr.: Moral and Cultural Leader

Great men are they who see that the spiritual is stronger than any material force—that thoughts rule the world.

—Ralph Waldo Emerson

*T*he stature of a man recedes into remoteness and myth as time goes by. Later generations start to take the figure for granted unless they can translate and forgive the traits and foibles of a bygone age and uncover what is of permanence behind what changes with the times. And that is all the more true in modern times. To those born in the 1980s or after, the 1950s already seem like another era.

In the month of February, two of our most revered presidents were born: George Washington on the twenty-second and Abraham Lincoln on the twelfth, seventy-seven years later. Many states, being able to celebrate the holidays as they saw fit, chose to also honor Lincoln along with Washington, renaming the celebration Presidents' Day.

Lincoln's legacy marked another step in a national reassessment of values. He was the one who brought to pass "a more complete union," an extension of political rights to all American citizens. The legacy of Washington was thus enlarged, and it is interesting to notice that again it was one man most of all who played a significant part in this.

Whether we celebrate Washington's Birthday or Presidents' Day, it is most significant to notice the human tendency to look to exceptional individuals, to what could be called the power of one, that is, the power of one fully expressed individuality, which can change the tides of time. Thus, it was only normal that the nation turned to yet another individual, who more than anyone else changed the meaning and experience of what it was to be an American in the twentieth and twenty-first centuries. And thus the nation saw the birth of yet another national holiday.

Washington lived fully within the eighteenth century, and Lincoln in the nineteenth century. Their successor lived a short life within the twentieth century. As we move back in time from late February to early February, and then from February to January, while moving forward one century at each step, we arrive at Martin Luther King Jr. Day on January 15 and commemorate a second individual who has given his life for something of importance to his country.

Washington lived sixty-seven years and was a two-term president; Lincoln barely initiated his second-term presidency and died at age fifty-six. Martin Luther King Jr., although he was a revered moral authority, never held office and died at age thirty-nine. Lincoln saw his task as continuing George Washington's work in addressing the slavery issue, which had been left as an open wound in the Constitution. With prescience, in leaving Springfield, Illinois, after twenty-five years, Lincoln addressed the crowd, expressing that he had a task as large as that of Washington's to undertake.

King was an admirer of Lincoln and was aware of the parallel themes of the Civil War and civil rights. The Emancipation Proclamation occurred on January 1, 1863. King asked President John Kennedy to offer a second Emancipation Proclamation exactly a century later. In Montgomery, Alabama, after the successful march from Selma along the Jefferson Davis Highway, King was returning to the cradle of the Confederacy. As author Stephen B. Oates points out, the march went up Dexter Avenue to the capitol, where Jefferson Davis had taken the oath of office as president of the Confederacy.[1] Like his predecessors, King worked at changing the consciousness of a nation. The first of our great presidents understood that the time had passed for monarchy and that the will of the people had to find its way into a new social compact. Lincoln understood that there could no longer be first-class and second-class citizens. And King worked at making that aspiration ever more concrete, fighting against segregation and the sociopolitical and economic forces that were obstacles to real equality.

Martin Luther King Jr. Day

The campaign for a federal holiday in King's honor began soon after his death in 1968. John Conyers (Democrat representative from Michigan) and Edward Brooke (Republican senator from Massachusetts) introduced a bill in Congress to make King's birthday a national holiday. Fifteen years later, Ronald Reagan reluctantly signed the holiday into law, and it was first observed on January 20, 1986. However, it was officially observed in all states of the Union for the first time only in 2000. The petition for Congress to pass the law for the holiday collected six million signatures and was one of the largest, if not the largest, petition in US history.

What did George Washington, Abraham Lincoln, and Martin Luther King Jr. have in common? They all strove for self-knowledge and self-improvement, seeing personal change and growth as parallel to the raising of consciousness that the nation needed. The United States would have been a different country had Washington not turned down a crown and confined his power in office to two terms, stepping down from power voluntarily as few or none had ever done before him. And we may not have a nation as we know it had Lincoln not preserved it with his life.

Martin Luther King Jr. realized that there was a power higher than the political, a power that could impress itself upon the political process and reignite the American dream. He called the nation to a complete reassessment of values. Let us see how his worldview significantly differed from that of many who were around him.

Promoting Cultural Power

Before many of the civil rights leaders, and more completely than anyone else, King understood he had a role distinct from and complementary to that of politicians. His relationships with presidents Kennedy and Johnson illustrate how unique were his positions at the time and how different from those of many other civil rights leaders. King knew that both parties were hypocritical and opportunistic in matters of civil rights and that only external pressure would influence outcomes. This is particularly why King refused to listen to warnings about bad political timing in many of his campaigns. He knew it would never be the right time if he had to listen to and subordinate himself to the political agenda. But this is not to say that King despised the political process; he only wanted to be an independent and equal player with it.

On January 22, 1960, King met with Senator John F. Kennedy, who was the front-runner candidate for the Democratic presidential nomination. From that day on until Kennedy was elected, King refused to endorse him, in spite of his favorable feelings. It was thanks to both John and Robert Kennedy that King was freed on October 28, 1960, when he had been jailed in Atlanta on the pretext that he had missed renewal of his driver's license. King's praise for the courage of Senator Kennedy was the closest he came to endorsing him, and the episode gave Kennedy critical black votes to win the election. Soon after Kennedy's election, however, King was throwing his weight around to influence Washington policy.

Refraining from endorsing Kennedy, King commented, "I feel someone must remain in the position of nonalignment, so that he can look objectively at both parties and be the conscience of both—not the servant or master of either."[2] In doing so, King naturally continued the intellectual trajectory he had started as a youth, following what could be called Hegelian dialectics, the ability always to seek the third and central element between two extreme but false alternatives—between capitalism and socialism, between contemplation and action, between individual and social responsibility, and so forth.

King's Hegelian Dialectics

In his studies, King had dedicated considerable energy to defining his Christian position. He first came across Walter Rauschenbusch, an engaged Christian social activist. Through him King came to the Rousseau-like idea of evil as the product of a capitalist society and its laws. This satisfied his need to see religion be active not only in personal salvation, but also in social change. At this juncture, King still seemed to be an advocate of Protestant liberalism. However, life circumstances led him to growing doubts about the goodness of human nature (which he had not initially questioned), and he turned his attention to the thinking of Reinhold Niebuhr to elucidate the matter. Niebuhr attacked liberal thinking, particularly its naïve optimism about human nature. For the same reasons, he attacked pacifism. King decided he had held onto a naïve belief in the power of reason and later agreed that reason needed to be accompanied by faith in order to change human nature.

His next goal was to reconcile the rift between idealism and relativism. He found such a synthesis in personalism, a personal idealism that sees the work of God at the level of the individual, justifying the belief in the inherent value of all human beings. At the end of this trajectory of the mind, he arrived at the conclusion that evil lives at the individual level, but that it can be transformed.

In order to deepen his understanding of personalism, King studied the divergent views of Paul Tillich and Henry Nelson Wieman in the research for his PhD, pitting transcendence in the first against immanence in the second. As a true Hegelian, King saw both the valid points and the limits of each view. He felt that Tillich's stance made individuality an empty proposition. Wieman's views could not offer concepts for the unity of the whole. King concluded that "a more adequate view is to hold a quantitative pluralism and a qualitative monism. In this way oneness and many-ness are preserved"[3] The results of this evolving thinking are clearly present in King's later spiritual growth.

Moving from studies to social action, King adapted his Hegelian thinking to the campaign for civil rights. Although he was neither the first nor the only one to advocate nonviolence, he was the one who gave it its full moral and spiritual significance. Already in his days at Morehouse College, he had come across the thoughts of Thoreau and had been inspired by the idea of the creative minority. Years later, he had the opportunity to hear a lecture about Gandhi by Mordecai W. Johnson, who argued that nonviolence could be effective in the United States as well. Gandhi had moved Thoreau's ideas further. Through Ghandi, King understood how anger can be rechanneled toward love. Thus inspired, King gradually embraced nonviolence as a tool that could work at the level of groups and nations. In nonviolence, King saw not just a strategy, but a tool for education and spiritual redemption. First of all, nonviolent resistance was the Hegelian solution to the conundrum between passive submission and violent resistance. Nonviolence requires much more courage than aggression and achieves the concrete results that passive acceptance could never exact from the oppressor. But ultimately much more was hoped for—and achieved.

During the civil rights era, many experienced a turnaround through the exposure to nonviolence, the oppressed no less than many oppressors. Nonviolence in King's terms actually embraces complete forgiveness in the recognition of the spiritual kernel present in every individual, even those who may be deemed unforgivable. "Forgiveness," King said, "does not mean ignoring what has been done or putting a false label on an evil act. It means, rather, that the evil act no longer remains as a barrier to the relationship.... While abhorring segregation, we shall love the segregationist. This is the only way to create the beloved community."[4]

MLK and JFK

Operating from a more encompassing position than pure political calculation, King could meet President Kennedy as an equal. In private, King once told Kennedy that he did not want to be in a position to be unable to criticize him if he thought Kennedy were wrong. Kennedy replied that it often helped him to be pushed. This exchange aptly sums up an optimal relationship that can be attained between a moral/cultural figure and a committed political figure. This is what each one of them could achieve given their respective spheres of influence. Kennedy's hands were tied to the proceedings of Congress. King could work toward a national climate that offered support to the president's executive power. Thus, for example, in the fall and winter of 1962, in the time leading to the centenary of Lincoln's Emancipation Proclamation, King wrote a series of articles to put pressure on President Kennedy.

In 1963, the Birmingham campaign of boycotts, sit-ins, and marches marked a turning point in the amount and intensity of involvement from the local community, and King's popularity surged among blacks and their leaders. Robert and John Kennedy supported King's results by planning to make desegregation a matter of fact. To do this, Robert Kennedy had to prevail over all other cabinet members. President Kennedy gave a national address on civil rights on June 11, 1963, and King had strong words of praise for the president. The success of Birmingham further spawned a score of nonviolent direct action campaigns in about nine hundred cities in the South, accompanied by demonstrations in their support by the rest of the country.

The Civil Rights Bill was written to begin desegregation of the schools and to deprive segregated facilities of federal funds. King harbored no illusions about the power of legislation alone to instill brotherhood. However, he knew that legislation was an important piece in making a transition possible: "It may be true that you cannot legislate integration, but you can legislate desegregation. It may be true that you cannot legislate morality, but behavior can be regulated. It may be true that the law cannot make a man love me, but it can restrain him from lynching me."[5] In this possibility lay the reason for his cooperation with political power, which he saw as capable of having the last word, but not able to initiate effective and durable change.

When President Kennedy was assassinated in November 1963, King expressed how deeply shaken he was and how much that made him turn to the thought of his own mortality. In early 1964, Kennedy's Civil Rights Bill passed the House, but faced opposition and filibuster in the Senate. King realized that more civil rights campaigns were necessary. This need found a culmination in the events of March 1965 in Selma and the attack on James Reeb, who fell into a coma and later died. This crime was a rallying cry for the nation, and calls were heard for federal troops to be sent to Selma. The event also gave President Johnson the support he needed to pass the bill. Johnson gave a special message on domestic legislation, the first time such a thing had been done in nineteen years. He was, in effect, conceding much that King had fought for. Johnson literally sounded like King in his oratory, finishing with, "We shall overcome."

MLK and President Johnson

Johnson also offered another great speech hailing "equality as a fact and result."[6] At this point there was great friendship between the two national figures. President Johnson signed the voting bill into law in the East Room, where Lincoln had signed the First Confiscation Act, seizing all slaves. The new act outlawed literacy tests and all other obstacles to voting rights. It appointed examiners to register those previously kept off the rolls. Most political analysts attributed the success to King's Selma campaign. The pattern of southern politics was altered forever.

King exerted a remarkable independence of mind, most of all in his views on Vietnam. These formed the basis for a whole new expansion of his dream. This was possible, first of all, because King did not ride the wave of dangerous political alliances. At this time, and with great courage, he distanced himself from Johnson's Vietnam policy. At the time of near-hysterical anticommunism, it took great courage to speak out against the administration's policies, and even King's staff was deeply divided on the matter. King, however, linked racial injustice and poverty to the Vietnam War, and national opposition rose immediately against him, as early as 1965.

In contrast to King's position, the National Association for the Advancement of Colored People (NAACP) unanimously opposed the effort to link the civil rights and peace issues. King was opposed not only by Roy Wilkins of the NAACP, but also by figures such as Whitney Young of the Urban League, Norman Thomas of the Socialist Party, and prominent civil rights activist Bayard Rustin, to name a few. Newspapers that had spoken glowingly about King now reversed their praises. Where others showed their vision to be limited by their political entanglements, King maintained a remarkable independence of mind and developed an encompassing vision. Moreover, he showed that he could learn from what the most extreme political fringes were saying, without adopting their extreme means or strategies. King remained, therefore, an unusual blend of radical visionary and moderate activist.

This trajectory was an escalation of the dream he had articulated in 1963 in Washington, DC. The original dream concerned America's civil rights and racial justice, the dream of the "beloved community." After 1963 this vision grew larger and embraced blacks and poor whites together, adding the concerns for economic justice, peace, disarmament, and the economic liberation of the third world. This was an understanding of the more systemic ills of the capitalistic system, of the global dimension and interrelatedness of the ills of a world economy running amok. In his early understanding of globalization, King prophetically defined the separate role that can be attributed to a civil society that hardly knew itself as such. He clearly attributed to this civil society a role independent and complementary to that of political action. King's approach reconciled personal consciousness and growth with political and cultural change. It is not surprising to realize, therefore, that King underwent true spiritual tests.

From the Depths to the Heights: Two Sides of King

King was a deeply tormented soul to the last. He knew very well that the King he knew was only a pale shadow of the King people saw. His greatness lay in his striving to change and in his great determination to face tremendous fear without retreating. Not least of all, he intuited that we cannot promote collective change without the willingness to shoulder a great part of the burden personally. In that, he was a modern Hiawatha, who knew himself to be both an individual of great capacities and a cannibal. King's cannibalism took the form of sexual behavior.

The All-Too-Human King

Soon after the 1963 March on Washington, King had invited men and women friends to his suite at the Willard Hotel. The FBI eavesdropped on sexual activity in King's room and later used the tapes to defame the leader. Similar allegations surfaced at other times. At the time of the Selma campaign, the FBI intimidated King through recordings that highlighted his womanizing. King felt that the tape was a warning from God because he had fallen short of his responsibilities in relation to the role he was fulfilling.

King was aware of not being a messiah or savior. His friends knew that he was very, very human. By his own admission, he was a troubled soul—troubled not only by the state of the world, but also by the state of his own soul waging its inner conflicts. "I am conscious of two Martin Luther Kings ... The Martin Luther King people talk about seems foreign to me." King had reached some deeper insights into human nature when he said, "Each one of us is two selves ... The great burden of life is always to keep that higher self in command. Don't let the lower self take over."[7] He acknowledged toward the end of his life that there is "a Mr. Hyde and a Dr. Jekyll in us ... I am a sinner like all God's children."[8] This was said in relation to his sexual infidelities.

King's Spiritual Experiences

When King was young, the greatest challenge lay in putting into action the belief in the immortality of the soul that he had already acquired, at least intellectually, at age seventeen or eighteen. In relation to this, we can trace a crescendo of spiritual experiences that are well documented. There were three major experiences that can be seen as marking his growth: the first and second close in time, respectively in 1956 and 1957, the third in the days preceding his death. These experiences accompanied attempts on his life and bombings. In between these was a barely unsuccessful attempt by a mentally unstable woman, who stabbed King and came close to severing his aorta. These marking episodes bear great similarities among themselves, and in them we can see an intensification of King's spiritual experiences.

In January 1956, after the police started harassing the Montgomery carpool, they also arrested King for speeding. In jail for the first time, King was prey to very strong emotions. Due to pressure exerted from his supporters gathering outside the jail, King was released and scheduled to return for his trial. At this point started the threats of hate letters, often signed "KKK," obscene phone calls, and more. King felt very jumpy, scared, and guilty about submitting his family to these ordeals. He started considering an honorable way to get out and turned to prayer.

He reports that he felt something like a presence, stirring in him. And it seemed that an inner voice was speaking to him with quiet assurance: "Martin Luther King, stand up for righteousness. Stand up for justice. Stand up for truth. And, lo, I will be with you, even unto the end of the world."[9] He saw lightning flash and heard thunder roar. It was the voice of Jesus telling him to still fight on. And "He promised never to leave me, never to leave me alone. No, never alone." Coming out of this experience, he felt stronger and had the energy to face the coming days. He realized, "I can stand up without fear. I can face anything." The calming presence brought home the experience of the personal God he had so long sought to understand. The meeting point of transcendence and immanence that he had struggled to apprehend in his PhD research was coming a step closer to immediate experience.

Soon after his arrest, King's house and church in Montgomery were bombed. Moreover, after that victory, the city ordered the bus company shut down. This brought back ghosts of guilt. In this state of mind, King went to the church service of January 15, 1957, the date of his twenty-eighth birthday.

King was still deeply affected by the events and for the first time broke down in public during a church service. He called for prayer but was unable to pray. Two ministers came to him and embraced him, and for several minutes he was unable to move. Finally they helped him to sit down. King explained, "Unexpectedly, this episode brought me great relief."[10] During the prayer he expressed his hope that there would be no killings and that if someone needed to die, it would be him. The event probably allowed him to relieve himself of accumulated guilt for believing he had caused all that suffering. Once again he felt God beside him, and he felt he could relinquish the fear of dying. This is what he expressed on January 27, after various other bombings and after an unexploded bomb had been found on the porch of his house: "Tell Montgomery that they can keep bombing and I'm going to stand up to them. If I had to die tomorrow morning I would die happy, because I've been to the mountaintop and I've seen the promised land; and it's going to be here in Montgomery."[11]

The first two episodes found a culmination in the days preceding King's death. At this stage of his activism, King wanted to highlight all kinds of social discrimination. But the plan of the next march on Washington was so grandiose and risky that many of his people and former supporters doubted its wisdom. King had in mind a Poor People's Campaign with an Economic Bill of Rights and wanted the nonviolent operation to last three months or longer. This attempt was his way to forge a Christian path that would be neither capitalism nor socialism, an old dream that had awakened during his studies.

King announced his new campaign on December 4, 1967, but his mood remained deeply pessimistic. He was caught between the tragic and explosive dimension of the race question, and the need to act boldly to spare further tragedy to his country. He also felt increasingly guilty for his personal sins and the toll they took on him and the movement, and many times in private he now spoke of the likelihood of death. It was almost always present in his mind and put him under great strain, causing him to be unable to sleep. In spite of all of this, he did not slow down. He was distressed by the lack of support within his own ranks, and in reality, he was also apprehensive of how the operation could turn out.

In February 1968, King was still under great strain. According to his colleagues, he was acting strangely, such as when he repeated his self-eulogy ("A Drum Major for Justice") to Abernathy on a plane to Acapulco. He was in what others described as a recurring depression, and displaying a sense of doom. In his public appearances, however, he called himself an optimist and was secure in his knowledge that "God loves us. He has not worked out a design for our failure."[12]

King had become involved in the protests of the black sanitation workers in Memphis, Tennessee, with whom Mayor Henry Loeb had no desire to negotiate. King was enthusiastic about the link he was forming between this cause and his planned upcoming march on Washington. He had entered the fray in Memphis without being told about the local problems, particularly the violent fringes of the protest.

On March 28 he led a march that turned out to have some very unruly participants. When riots erupted with smashing and looting, King announced that he refused to lead a violent march. He called it off, but the violence continued; by the end, it had affected some 150 stores, one youth had been killed, and sixty people had been injured. King was upset because of this and because he had been kept in the dark about potential violence. These events also threatened the public perception of his upcoming planned march on Washington. A mass meeting in which he planned to speak had to be canceled. Besieged by guilt, he could not manage to sleep. He desperately wanted to come back later to Memphis to lead another march with the same factions that had resorted to violence previously. He perceived this as crucial for his future plans. He announced that he would be back in town between the third and the fifth of April. As King had feared, the press linked the failure of the march to the risks of the projected Poor People's Campaign. They were linking his presence to the likelihood of riots.

During those days, King continued to feel very depressed. Still, he was fighting all he could to convince his staff to return to Memphis, and they finally came around to his support. It was around this time that President Johnson declined to seek reelection, and the nation could see the growing charisma of Robert Kennedy. King took great strength from these signs. He felt that Kennedy would take a stance on Vietnam and favor the Poor People's Campaign, or at least help create a supportive atmosphere around it.

On April 3, King, depressed and fearful about ta poor turnout, did not want to offer another speech, and initially asked Abernathy to speak for him. When Abernathy showed up, it was clear that the crowd clamored for King, and the faithful friend managed to persuade him to rise to the occasion. King said that if God had offered him a choice of a time to live in, strangely enough he would have chosen "a few years in the second half of the twentieth century," because "only when it's dark enough can you see the stars"[13] He recalled when he had been stabbed in New York ten years earlier. He evoked the sit-ins and the Freedom Rides, the fights of Albany and of Birmingham, the "I Have a Dream" speech, the movement in Selma and up to the present in Memphis. One cannot help but wonder if King was retracing the life tableau that a person sees upon dying.

And this went even further with the words, "Now, it doesn't really matter what happens now … because I've been to the mountaintop…. and I've seen the Promised Land…. I'm not worried about anything. I'm not fearing any man. 'Mine eyes have seen the glory of the coming of the Lord' … I have a dream this afternoon that the brotherhood of man will become a reality." And he finished, "Free at last! Free at last! God Almighty, free at last!"[14] The speech was both a foreshadowing of death and an affirmation of life. After all, he had previously reasserted, "I want to live". After this speech, King broke through his despair again.

King's Relevance for the Future of America

To the last, King was faithful to a new American dream, and everything he expressed expanded the dimension of that dream, which more and more took the dimension of the "beloved community" or "the brotherhood of man." With one foot Martin Luther King stood in the aspirations of his time; with another he stepped into intuited horizons and dreams to come. His relationship with Marxism/Socialism shows how aspects of both present and future intertwined. On the one hand, he saw in the Marxist early thinkers people with a fiery devotion to social justice. He did not fall into the trap, or the political intimidation, of anticommunism. He saw it for what it truly was—a smoke screen paralyzing people into false alternatives, a blank check used to justify excesses and discourage free inquiry.

Given his spiritual leanings that held him at arm's length from Marxist theory, he looked for a synthesis between capitalism and socialism from a rather pragmatic standpoint. His views turned toward something like the Swedish social-democratic model, in which he saw no striking poverty and a consistent safety net for the underprivileged. He saw in it a socially conscious democracy, which reconciles the truths of individualism and collectivism. From the theoretical perspective he was closer to Niebuhr, who married Marxist historical analysis of the facts with the social message of the gospels. This much is true of King, the pragmatic thinker. On the other hand, the visionary in him showed further prophetic paths toward a future that is yet to emerge.

Reaching beyond Capitalism and Socialism

King's analysis of the limitations of Marxism also reached further than most in his time could see. "Karl Marx got messed up, first because he didn't stick with the Jesus he had read about; but secondly because he didn't even stick with Hegel."[15] This sums up King's deeper convictions. The first objection points to Marx's little-known early interest in Christianity and the personal battle that had thrown him into atheism and materialism. The second and deeper objection is the recognition of Marxism's dualistic thinking, the antithesis to King's Hegelian threefold thinking. Overcoming this dualistic and polarized thinking is something that goes beyond the postulation of a tame social-democratic compromise as the future horizon of humankind.

It is in King's most intuitive and prophetic utterances that this future aspect found expression. When he spoke of systemic ills, he also offered a vision of what a new culture would need to rise toward. "We, as a nation, must undergo *a radical revolution of values*. When machines and computers, profit and property rights are considered more important than people, the *giant triplets of racism, materialism, and militarism* are incapable of being conquered."[16] Note here that the revolution of values stands in contrast to materialism, among other things. This was certainly not a commonly held view in his time.

More prophetic still, and very timely for the new millennium's social activism, are King's intimations of what a new world would imply. Already in Montgomery he had invited his followers to place the terms of choice into a wider perspective: "We stand today between two worlds— the dying order and the emerging new. By resisting nonviolently the negro can speed up the coming of the new world."[17] And at the Prayer Pilgrimage for Freedom (May 17, 1957), he stated, "If we indulge in hate, the new order will only be the old order."[18] In his view, time was running out for America, for nonviolence, and for the new moral order. One can trace biblical origins in this restated vision. It corresponds nevertheless to an eminently practical rejection of all extremism or utopian ideals, a complete alignment of means and ends, a call for a powerful imagination that cuts across political thinking, a call to link personal and social change, all of this giving new possibilities to the American dream. Nonviolence itself was central to this reassessment of values. And the American dream took yet another dimension in King's vision. He saw in the United States the land in which the experiment of the integration of all races could first take place worldwide. He feared that if what he called the "beloved community" failed in America, it would equally fail the world over.

The full scope of King's vision is expressed in his messianic understanding of the global dimension of the crisis facing humanity. Let us turn once more to his words, to the repeated affirmation of the linked destiny of all people in the world. In an open letter to the white clergymen of Alabama, King said: "We are caught in an inescapable network of mutuality, tied in a single garment of destiny. Whatever affects one directly, affects all indirectly.... Anyone who lives inside the United States can never be considered an outsider anywhere within its bounds."[19] And at a 1967 Christmas sermon given at the Ebenezer Baptist

Church in Atlanta, he stated: "Before you finish eating breakfast in the morning, you've depended on more than half the world [for your food]. This is the way our universe is structured, this is its interrelated quality. We aren't going to have peace on earth until we recognize this basic fact of the interrelated structure of all reality."[20] In this, too, King stood as a moral force and a spiritual leader, with profound understanding of the terrific threats and the great promises that the future stands between.

The Power of One

Washington's Birthday, President's Day, and finally the latest personal holiday, Martin Luther King Jr. Day, honor the struggle for the recognition of the power that is present in each individual, which shines, in some cases more than others, to remind us of what it is to achieve a great measure of inner freedom, the freedom that unleashes the power of one. Washington, Lincoln, and King, each in his own time, brought something new and essential to the nation—a reassessment of values, an emergence of something different from what had preceded, if even in a small measure. This difference changed the culture around them. Washington accomplished a leadership of service and renunciation. King showed through nonviolence the achievement of an inner and outer freedom, deeper than had been thought possible until then. Both inner and outer are truly the power of one, in the sense of a Tamanend.

As a minister and a person versed in seeking a larger paradigm, King was truly a cultural hero, integrating social and spiritual activism. Nonviolence, coupled with a Hegelian dialectic that overcomes simple dualism, allies the strengths of consciousness movements to those of social movements, making them stronger than either alone. King's uncharacteristic inclusion (surprising to Americans) of the evils of materialism, along with racism and militarism, points to the larger dimension of the establishment of a new cultural power. At present, this is achieved by a growing civil society and movements that stand outside of the political arena, although they exert positive pressure on it. The appeal of a movement like Occupy Wall Street rests on such influence. But the strength of this cultural influence lies in letting the power of the whole emerge through the new practice of public consensus decision making, derived in large part from American Quakerism.

Toward a Revolution of Values

The evils of the social order are represented in America by a growing materialism, which is now entering an entrenched state of denial that disregards the growing social divides, the devastation of the environment, and the constant degradation of the individual. We can no longer remain materialists, seeking to resist recognition of a planet more and more mechanized, devastated, and reified. By doing so, Einstein would remind us, we remain within the logic of the paradigm we are trying to change. We can collectively cocreate a new future only by operating within an altogether different paradigm. Martin Luther King Jr. was one of the first to understand this reality, grope to define it, and design strategies for its attainment.

The new social order is exemplified, on the one hand, by the world of nanotechnology, genetic engineering, eugenics, artificial intelligence, and robotics, to name but a few of the mechanisms of elite globalization; on the other hand, by fundamentalisms of different stripes that seek only a personal nirvana, ascension, or rapture, detached from any larger understanding, while everything around us is careening toward destruction.

It is not a simple coincidence that in King we honor a preacher who was also a social activist. He was one because he was the other as well, and the strength of the one lent to the other, although King remained a divided soul himself. In that dividedness, he is a symbol of all modern Americans. But he understood, the first in his time to do so, that human rights and human dignity can best be anchored through placing the human being and his search for meaning beyond the world of matter and all hyper-materialistic pursuits of the present. Much of this appears in his last book *Where Do We Go from Here?: Chaos or Community?* in which King aptly summarizes the trajectory of his life. His conclusions push him to the outer limits of his Hegelian thinking:

> One of the great problems of mankind is that we suffer from
> a poverty of the spirit, which stands in glaring contrast to our

scientific and technological abundance. The richer we have become materially, the poorer we have become morally and spiritually.

Every man lives in two realms, the internal and the external. The internal is that realm of spiritual ends expressed in art, literature, morals, and religion. The external is that complex of devices, techniques, mechanisms, and instrumentalities by means of which we live. Our problem today is that we have allowed the internal to become the external. We have allowed the means by which we live to outdistance the ends for which we live. So much of modern life can be summarized in the suggestive phrase of Thoreau: "Improved means to an unimproved end." This is the serious predicament, the deep and haunting problem, confronting modern man. Enlarged material powers spell enlarged peril if there is not proportionate growth of the soul.[21]

Unique in his time, Martin Luther King Jr. could link the personal dimensions of the current cultural crisis to the political crisis that is intimately linked to it. This is what he communicated in the need for a revolution of values. In the same speech, King continued:

This revolution of values must go beyond traditional capitalism and communism. We must honestly admit that capitalism has often left a gulf between superfluous wealth and abject poverty.... Equally, communism reduces men to a cog in the wheel of the state. The communist may object, saying that in Marxist theory the state is an "interim reality" that will "wither away" when the classless society emerges. True—in theory; but it is also true that, while the state lasts, it is an end in itself. Man is a means to that end. He has no inalienable rights. His only rights are derived from, and conferred by, the state. Under such a system the fountain of freedom runs dry.... Truth is found neither in traditional capitalism nor in classical communism. Each represents a partial truth. Capitalism fails to see the truth in collectivism. Communism fails to see the truth in individualism. Capitalism fails to realize that life is social. Communism fails to realize that life is personal. The good and just society is neither the thesis of capitalism nor the antithesis of communism, but a socially conscious democracy which reconciles the truths of individualism and collectivism.[22]

Martin Luther King Jr., the thinker, had foreseen and begun to articulate the reality of a larger actor in the social arena, that of civil society as a force that can stand on its own, against the pressures and encroachments of allied political and economic powers, government, and corporations. It is only a different sector, separate both from the political and the economic, that can start to shape the search for meaning that is essential for cultural renewal. It is no wonder that the third sector has grown nationally and internationally to represent a counterpole to global governments and global business. As Paul Hawken has shown in *Blessed Unrest*, its presence is such that it has to be reckoned with worldwide. It is the source of that cultural power that can bring new meaning to our lives.

Washington, Lincoln, and Martin Luther King Jr.

It is curious, to say the least, how much continuity there is between Washington, Lincoln, and Martin Luther King Jr., and how each took on the continuation of the task of his predecessor. And it is only logical that this triad has been so present in the American soul that it has received official recognition in the holidays. At one level, freedom is possible only when the individual is not overshadowed by the powers of the state. And this is possible only when political power is countered by an equally strong, or stronger, independent cultural arena of expression. Paradoxically, this independent culture was much stronger at the time of the colonies than it is at present. Even understanding of the very notion of civil society as the fount of culture is dormant at present. The success of King, and his hold over the American psyche, is due in great part to his dimension as a unique moral and cultural leader. Many leaders grew into or out of the Civil Rights movement, but none forged an independent path for American civil society as clearly as did King. He alone remained completely independent of political alliances. As a representative of American culture, he had the freedom to speak of all the ills that besieged and still besiege American society. Not surprisingly, in him more than in anyone else, nonviolent activism signified a tool of cultural renewal for individuals and a nation, not just a strategic choice.

Washington, Lincoln, and Martin Luther King Jr., more than many others, have given shape to the United States, to its integrity as a nation, and thus they conditioned its culture. In them, the ideal of freedom found new expression. Washington seeded the values of a democratic republic, of the government of "We the People," of a complete departure from the pervasive, surviving culture of the divine right of monarchs. Lincoln showed that a nation could go through such an ordeal as one of the bloodiest civil wars in history and still preserve its form of government. He preserved the most important civil and national American values when they were threatened from the inside by the expansion of slavery and from the outside by the interference of foreign powers. Martin Luther King Jr. unveiled every aspect of the empire that our nation has become. He summoned our consciousness to a revolution of values, to the renewing of the dream of the beloved community.

Chapter 6

Women: The Long Struggle for Equality

What woman needs is not as a woman to act or rule, but as a nature to grow, as an intellect to discern, as a soul to live freely, and unimpeded to unfold such powers as were given her when we left our common home.

—Margaret Fuller

*T*wo national holidays that occur close together in the calendar mark the emergence of a new world consciousness: Mother's Day and Women's Day. Both had their origin in the United States, yet the first one found acceptance in other countries, strangely enough, before being partially readopted in the United States. And both offer complementary aspects of a larger phenomenon.

Julia Ward Howe wrote her famous "Battle Hymn of the Republic" after she met Abraham Lincoln at the White House in 1861, and her lyrics were one of the most popular songs of the Union during the Civil War. Years after, Howe had cause to reevaluate the consequences of war, and she turned her attention to pacifism and women's rights. Her Mother's Day proclamation of 1870 was not for honoring mothers, per se, but for organizing pacifist mothers against war. It was initially called an "Appeal to Womanhood throughout the World."

Unfortunately, Howe's proclamation did not result in a congress such as she requested. The modern holiday of Mother's Day had its symbolic origin in 1908, when Anna Jarvis held a memorial for her mother in Grafton, West Virginia. Jarvis just wanted to fulfill her mother's dream of making a celebration for all mothers. Her efforts to promote Mother's Day bore fruit in 1914, when President Wilson established the official national holiday. However, by the early 1920s, Jarvis was disappointed with the commercialization of the holiday, even though the holiday was adopted the world over.

In the same years, which were years of social and political ferment, another aspect of womanhood came to the fore: that of woman as a full participant in social affairs. It took the form of the first national Women's Day on February 28, 1909, and was the brainchild of the American Socialist Party. The idea had more success abroad than in the United States; international socialism took it further at the 1910 International Women's Conference that preceded the Second Socialist International in Copenhagen. March 18, 1911, was celebrated in women's honor in the German-speaking countries (Germany, Austria, Switzerland) and Denmark. The date was subsequently moved to March 8.

What started in America with two holidays corresponded to a cosmopolitan yearning, a need to reconnect with ancient roots of the soul. Celebrations of mothers and motherhood had occurred throughout the world in ancient times. The Greek had a cult to Cybele, a sort of great mother, the Romans to Hilaria (Cybele's Roman name).

Renewing the Declaration Seventy-Two Years Later

"We hold these truths to be self-evident,…" This famous phrase rang out for a second time at a convention in Seneca Falls, New York, in 1848, seventy-two years after the Declaration of Independence. This time the words were spoken not in Philadelphia, but in upstate New York; not by delegates from the colonies, but by a group of women and men. And two new words were added to the sentence: "… that all men *and women* are created equal." It would take yet another seventy-two years to bring that proclamation to fruition. The new declaration, which is now commonly called the "Declaration of Rights and Sentiments," came into being as part of a women's convention.

The idea of a women's convention surfaced at a tea party on July 9 or 10, 1848, at Jane Hunt's house in Seneca Falls. Jane Hunt had invited Lucretia Mott and Elizabeth Cady Stanton, among others. All but Elizabeth Stanton were Quakers, originally from the Philadelphia area. Elizabeth had moved to Seneca Falls in 1847.

At the party the conversation turned to the topic of women's rights, and Elizabeth spoke with great passion. The five women resolved to hold a convention, and to do it right away, while the Quaker minister Lucretia Mott would be in the area, since her name played a critical role in attracting a crowd. Frederick Douglass was invited and responded favorably.

A meeting to plan the convention took place a few days later. The women wanted to draft a declaration and had some models to draw from. No existing models appealed to them until they started reading the Declaration of Independence. They decided to modify the preamble and rewrite the whole; it is generally acknowledged that Elizabeth Stanton played the leading role in this.

It seems that the spirit of Philadelphia and Quakerism were present not far from the events; all of this was taking place in a geographic area that was in the heart of the old Iroquois confederacy. There was an extended period of gestation, even before the tea party that led to the Seneca Falls Convention. The path is worth retracing.

A previous event that laid the foundation for the Seneca Falls Women's Convention had occurred eight years earlier at the London 1840 World Anti-Slavery Convention. Eight of the US delegates to the convention were female, in a group formed mostly by men. The women were denied equal participation in the proceedings and had to witness the events silently, from behind curtains. At the meeting, Lucretia Mott and Elizabeth Stanton forged a lasting friendship. Elizabeth admired the Quaker minister, who was more than twenty years her elder. Together they planned for further collaboration, but things did not progress in the way they hoped.

In 1842, Elizabeth gave birth to her first child, and other children followed. Her husband was rarely at home, and she did not have time to plan any events. But later, when the circumstances were right, things happened quickly, like a wildfire. The event that took eight years to conceive and gestate found a resolution in two weeks. And Seneca Falls, where Elizabeth had just moved, turned out to be the perfect place. It was a very progressive town, with a ferment of revivalism, spiritualism, communitarianism, temperance, and abolition. In addition, a good number of Quakers had moved there in the twenties and thirties. And, as the name indicates, Seneca Falls rests in the heart of the old Iroquois confederacy.

In 1848 this important movement for equality was born in North America, a movement that would have great importance for the world. And the spirit of the Declaration of Independence and of the Constitutional Convention lived on. Civility in the debates was the hallmark of the first meetings; much of that was owed to the Quakers' insistence on having all voices heard. This civility served the movement well, because the process would last another seventy-two years after Seneca Falls. It has been estimated that to get the word *male* out of the Constitution, there had to be: fifty-six campaigns of referenda; 480 suffrage amendments submitted to the vote; 277 attempts to have woman suffrage in the party conventions; "thirty campaigns to get presidential nominating conventions to adopt woman suffrage planks in party platforms; and nineteen campaigns with nineteen successive congresses."[1] All of this was done without advocates from within the structures of power.

Forging the Triumvirate

An exceptional individual was the catalyst for the Seneca Falls Convention; she was a woman all looked up to, and few could find fault with. Although women's rights formed only part of her life concerns, she remained a compass and a rudder in the long and stormy path to women's equality.

After a brief career as a teacher, Lucretia Mott became a Quaker minister in 1821, at age twenty-eight. She was one of the very few women in the clergy, though not the first among the Quakers. True to her tradition, her sermons emphasized the inner light, the presence of the divine spark within each individual. And her life was a constant witness to it. An ardent abolitionist since her youth, she had joined the "free produce" movement, advocating the idea of buying only products not produced by slaves. From its inception, she was a member of the American Anti-Slavery Society, which her husband had helped to found. What a person of her character could achieve at that time was truly remarkable. She was the only woman to speak at the Anti-Slavery Society's organizational meeting in Philadelphia. Not content with this daring, after the convention, Mott and other women, both black and white, founded the Philadelphia Female Anti-Slavery Society, a uniquely integrated organization for the times. The society developed close ties to Philadelphia's black community, in whose churches Mott often preached.

Mott's and Elizabeth Stanton's friendship endured. The elder woman was often the one who could recall the younger, more impatient sister to reason and moderation in times of need.

Three major protagonists in the struggle for women's rights were born within five years of each other and within 150 miles, from Jonestown, New York to West Stockbridge, Massachusetts. The oldest was Elizabeth Cady Stanton, born in 1815, in Jonestown, New York; the youngest, Susan Brownell Anthony, was born in 1820 in Adams, Massachusetts, just the other side of the border from New York. Together the two have been hailed as the fulcrum figures of the women's movement. Lucy Stone played a very important role as well and is mentioned alongside the others in what has been called the women's triumvirate. The lives of these three remarkable individuals were closely intertwined in other ways, in addition to their birthplaces and dates; they were obviously drawn together by subtle and recurring life themes. The fate of their coming together, parting ways, and reuniting marked the whole movement of women's rights. Over time they created two parallel and partly rival movements—Susan B. Anthony and Elizabeth Cady Stanton on one hand, Lucy Stone on the other—that took some twenty years to come to reconciliation.

The Road to Change

Much was happening in the nineteenth century that would forever change the face of the nation. None would be more affected than women. The first decades, especially in the Northeast, were marked by men abandoning farming and taking jobs in the cities and towns. This left more women alone at home, and their work became all the more important. However, in time, another significant trend was women's enrollment in the workforce, particularly in the growing industrial Northeast. It was no surprise that women's wages were considerably lower than those of men, and women had hardly any access to the professions, other than teaching. Women teachers were paid less than half what men were; most, if not all, administrators were male.

Some professions were slowly opening up to women; in medicine Elizabeth Blackwell, Lucy Stone's future sister-in-law, graduated from Geneva College, New York, in 1849. Few church denominations allowed women to become ministers; Quakers were the rare exception.

Social reform and activism were the hallmark of the new century. Mothers and women, who had been held responsible for the moral well-being of their families, now turned their gaze to the larger community by founding schools for the poor and assisting widows and orphans, the physically impaired, and the new waves of immigrants. This social interest and unrest blossomed most strongly in the Northeast and in urban areas in the West.

A woman's legal status differed considerably depending on whether she were married or single, according to the prevailing code of law, the so-called Blackstone's Law. When married, the woman became identified with the man, relinquishing claim to all property she had brought into the marriage. The single woman retained her property, but at the cost of a stigma that was hard to bear and of very limited opportunities for sustaining herself. De facto, most spinsters would likely be condemned to live with close family. Divorce rates were starting to rise, and some states offered more grounds for breaking the marriage.

Yet something was changing in regard to women's access to higher education, and to culture in general, that would set an irreversible trend. Women's education was spurred through the forming of hundreds of female academies and seminaries. Among great educators of this time were Catharine Beecher, the oldest of the sisters who founded the Hartford Female Seminary; Mary Lyon, who founded the Mount Holyoke Female Seminary; and Emma Hart Willard, founder of Troy Female Seminary, New York.

Lucy Stone graduated from Oberlin—one of the few coeducational colleges; she was the first woman from Massachusetts to graduate from college. Prior to being accepted at Oberlin, she had tried, unsuccessfully, to enroll in the Troy Female Seminary, which was closer to her home. So did Susan B. Anthony, but neither was able to obtain a scholarship. Elizabeth Cady Stanton did enroll; ironically, she never finished her studies.

Lucy Stone: Knowing the Full Plight of Women

Lucy Stone set a number of precedents in women's history. She was the first woman from Massachusetts to graduate from college, and she achieved this through great personal sacrifice. And she was the first one to keep her maiden name after marriage. Others who did the same after her were known as Lucy Stoners. Elizabeth Cady Stanton was born to wealth; Susan B. Anthony was born to a progressive and supportive Quaker family. Neither of them had to overcome the obstacles that were commonly set in the way of women in the same way that Lucy Stone did.

Lucy was born in 1818 in a farming family, the eighth of nine children. Her father, an alcoholic, was the violent, feared, and unbending patriarch of tradition. Poverty obliged all the children to supplement the family income; the boys hunted and fished, and the girls sewed and wove or canned fruits. Together they milked or attended to the cows. The mother lived in fear of the father; she had to beg him for money or occasionally steal. Seeing her mother's dignity so affected remained engraved in Lucy's mind.

The Congregationalist Church interpreted the Bible in favor of the status quo, no differently from most of the others, upholding the subservient position of women. Lucy believed, deep in her heart, that this was interpretation, not tradition, and vowed to read the Bible in the Greek and Latin originals, confirming her insights when she finally did. And she was not accustomed to hiding her thoughts when she came to question authority. The first chance arose when she started teaching at age sixteen. Having noticed that she was paid less than half the male teacher she had replaced, she raised her voice. She received a modest increase. No doubt she noticed she could speak her mind and effect some measure of change. And the course was set for more.

In 1838, she enrolled at Mount Holyoke's Female Seminary at her own expense. Lucy's thirst for knowledge was sparked by studies in algebra, geography, logic, literature, and more. At that time she had already been awakened to the issue of slavery and had started reading *The Liberator* by William Lloyd Garrison. She had barely had time to whet her intellectual appetite when she had to return home to care for the daughters of her just-deceased sister Eliza. The theme of attending to personal loss, which meant sacrificing personal or political goals, would return often later in her life. She returned to teaching and found the energy to continue her education in Latin, grammar, and mathematics from a private tutor and fellow abolitionist. Another loss followed after a short interval; her sister Rhoda died in 1839, and Lucy kept company with her grieving mother. In the time that she could spare, she continued to attend classes at private schools. Until 1843 Lucy took classes in local private schools; then she prepared her entrance examination for Oberlin College in Ohio.

Acceptance to college did not come with all the privileges we take for granted today. On the basis of specific passages from the Bible, women were not allowed to speak in public or address mixed audiences. Lucy, who could now finally read the Bible in the original, had established in her mind that the Bible was not at fault, but that it was "friendly to women." With Antoinette Brown—an abolitionist and suffragist who was studying to become a minister—she devoted herself to breaking taboos. The two formed a secret women's oratorical society that met in the woods. Eventually they married brothers and cemented a deep friendship. Still, Lucy wanted something more than the echo of the trees, so she spent three weeks preparing for her first speech at the local antislavery society. She delivered it to a mixed audience in August 1846.

On returning to Massachusetts, Lucy gave her first speech in October 1847 about women's rights, "The Province of Women." This, like all her other famous and successful speeches, was an extemporaneous, unwritten speech. The first to be struck by her qualities as an orator was William Lloyd Garrison, who approached her the same year, asking her to become a lecturer and organizer for his American Anti-Slavery Society. This was the beginning of Lucy Stone's public career.

At this point in the story entered a man who spent his later life fully devoted to women's rights. Henry Blackwell first saw Lucy Stone in

1851, from the gallery of the Massachusetts legislature, as she advocated an amendment to the state constitution proposing full civil rights to women. Henry, an abolitionist from a progressive family in Cincinnati, had other opportunities to see Stone speak on further occasions and was smitten by her aura. Doubting whether he could find an audience in her full schedule, Blackwell nevertheless managed to gain an introduction through William Lloyd Garrison. Feeling that he should lose no time, he proposed marriage to her within the hour. He began an irresistible two-year courtship that eventually yielded fruit.

The wedding was one of the most liberated of its time. The word *obey* was removed from the ritual, and the husband-to-be renounced his exclusive legal right to her property. Creating another precedent, the bride was the first in the United States to retain her maiden name. In joining the Blackwells, Lucy forged lasting ties with a group of freethinkers and reformers. She became allied with a powerful coterie of five women who pursued their individual interests with a passion. Ironically, all of them had given up marriage—a sacrifice Lucy had not made in coming to meet them.

Lucy gave birth to her child Alice in 1857. The stay-at-home mother was chronically depressed in the following years. This period coincided with the time of the Civil War, in which the struggle for women's rights lay dormant. However, she was able to attend the first meeting of the Women's Loyal National League in 1863 in New York—organized by Elizabeth Stanton and Susan B. Anthony.

1848 to 1852: A Coming Together

The years 1848 to 1852 marked a turning point for our friends in the triumvirate. Although Lucy Stone had not been able to attend the Seneca Falls convention in 1848, she nevertheless had an experience that year that provided a destiny turning point. While walking through Boston Commons, she stopped to admire the statue known as *The Greek Slave*. Breaking into tears, she had an epiphany, experiencing a parallel between this work of art and women's current condition. From that day on, she resolved to mention women's rights issues in her speeches alongside abolition. This presented a problem for most members of the

American Anti-Slavery Society, who did not want to mix the two issues. Presented with a request to discontinue speaking on the subject, Stone concluded that she must leave the society. A compromise was reached, in which Lucy was offered four dollars to speak solely of abolition on weekends. This left her free to speak of women's rights during the week.

This was 1848, the same year that the women at Seneca Falls called the first women's convention. And that event marked Elizabeth Cady Stanton's awakening to her mission. At the Seneca Falls Convention, she read her "Declaration of Rights and Sentiments." And Lucretia Mott's and Elizabeth's friendship reached a new milestone as well.

Lucretia Mott and Elizabeth Stanton met in Seneca Falls under the protective shadow of the old tree of the White Roots of Peace. It seemed that now, centuries later, the Iroquois impulse was nurturing a new step in society's evolution. The Motts were part of the Indian Committee of the Philadelphia Yearly Meeting of the Society of Friends, and at the time of her visit, Lucretia saw the Iroquois nation going through changes in their governance structure, with debates in which the women exercised their voice.[2] Nor was that the only thing Lucretia would have noticed. In Iroquois culture, women controlled their own property, whereas American women, once married, had no control over theirs. Iroquois women had responsibilities in ceremonies and ritual; American women could not speak in churches. Iroquois women had a balanced participation with men in family affairs, but American women were completely subordinate. Finally, Iroquois women could choose their leaders and hold political offices; American women could do nothing of the sort. Elizabeth Stanton was not alien to the Iroquois world. She ate meals with Oneida women in Peterboro, New York, during frequent visits to her social-activist cousin Gerrit Smith.[3]

On the first day of the Seneca Falls Convention, July 19, 1848, in addition to women, there were about forty men attending, and even a few mothers with their children. Elizabeth Stanton offered an initial address and followed it with the "Declaration of Rights and Sentiments," which was read slowly so questions could be answered and changes incorporated.

On the second day, after a new reading of the declaration, there was a vote, and the document was adopted unanimously. The eleven resolutions that come at the end of the document were reread and voted upon individually. The suffrage resolution was judged to be the most controversial of all. Even the elder Lucretia Mott and several other Quakers felt challenged by it, although Elizabeth stood firm on her ground. Interestingly, the day was saved by Frederick Douglass, who threw his weight behind the resolution.

The meeting brought to light substantial divergences and animated discussion, but even so, it was conducted with openness and decorum. Elizabeth Stanton called the atmosphere one of "religious earnestness." Some newspapers were more impressed with the orderly proceeding than with the ideas or results.

Lucy, Susan, and Elizabeth

In May 1850, Lucy Stone traveled to Boston to plan a national convention focusing on women's rights, to be held in Worcester, Massachusetts. Lucy was named secretary of the initiative. Shortly after notices went out, Lucy was called to nurse her cholera-infected brother Luther back to health. His wife, Phebe, was afraid to tend him, since she feared for her unborn baby. It was too late for Lucy to do anything other than accompany Luther through his death in July of that year. After the funeral, Lucy accompanied her sister-in-law back home. En route Phebe went prematurely into labor and delivered a stillborn son. While Lucy was caring for Phebe in a town of eastern Illinois, she contracted typhoid fever, battling on the brink of death for eighteen days. Her recovery took until October, barely allowing her to reach Massachusetts shortly before the opening session of the Worcester convention.

At the 1850 National Women's Rights Convention in Worcester, some thousand people showed up. There were delegates from eleven states, including one from the new state of California. Lucy Stone conserved her scant energy until the last meeting, when she took the stage. She spoke briefly in favor of women's property rights. This was such a moving speech that Horace Greeley, who witnessed it, mentioned it, reporting favorably on the events of the convention in his *New York Tribune*. Horace Greeley's particularly admiring description of Lucy Stone's speech became the turning point for Susan B. Anthony's involvement in women's rights. From that day she decided it would become her own life path; she never strayed from that resolve.

Now that the three women had found their place in the movement, things started to accelerate in the next two years. The meeting of Elizabeth Stanton and Susan B. Anthony was catalyzed through the key presence of Amelia Bloomer, in whose Seneca Falls House the two had already met in the fall of 1851. They had come to hear Garrison and the English abolitionist George Thompson. Looking back on that day, Elizabeth Stanton commented, "There she stood, with her good earnest face and genial smile ... the perfection of neatness and sobriety," and further, "I liked her thoroughly."[4] In the summer of 1852, Lucy Stone went to Seneca Falls to meet at Elizabeth's home and help draw up the charter for a proposed People's College. There she finally met Susan B. Anthony.

It is time to turn now to the most central collaboration of this story. No two individuals have offered a more significant contribution to the women's rights movement than Elizabeth Cady Stanton and Susan B. Anthony. And a great reason for this was in the way they complemented each other and worked together. They could not have been any more different, and yet they found their strength in those differences.

The polarity of their individualities appeared even at first sight. Due to her cheerfulness and natural vitality, Elizabeth's early nickname was "sunflower." Susan was tall and angular and stood in dignified uprightness. She was approached by the younger admirers as Aunt Susan, or in jest, even Saint Susan. She was committed, exacting, hardworking, sober, and overly serious. She had an iron will and constitution. Elizabeth, in contrast, praised the power of naps for intellectual stimulation and knew how to value the moment. She was short and tended to roundedness, the image of a jovial grandmother. In her presence one could forget cares and woes. More delicate of health, she suffered in her later years from arthritis, obesity, and probably diabetes. Susan was a tactician; Elizabeth was the philosopher.

Elizabeth Cady Stanton: the Jefferson of the Movement

In 1815, the year of Elizabeth's birth, two of her father Daniel Cady's sons had died: an infant and an eight-year-old. The same had happened four years earlier with the infant James. Daniel Cady was not to know the prized joy of fathering a boy to manhood, and his stern Presbyterianism was no solace against such blows of fate.

The Cady family had settled in Columbia County in upstate New York in the seventeenth century. Daniel had been first a schoolteacher, then a judge, and finally a politician. By 1798, he had moved to Jonestown, in the foothills of the Adirondacks. His wife, Margaret Livingston, was of Dutch aristocratic descent. She was constantly passing from childbirth to mourning, having given birth eleven times in twenty-six years, with five losses. From her affluent family, not surprisingly, Elizabeth inherited a sense of superiority and privilege, together with her very own determination toward freedom.

At the death of yet another son (Eleazar Livingston, at age twenty), Daniel Cady admitted to his eleven-year-old daughter Elizabeth that he wished she were a boy. On that occasion she promised her father that she would try to be all that he would have wanted from her brothers. Elizabeth was the third of the surviving daughters and a bit of a rebellious tomboy, trying her hand at running, riding, and playing chess as well as playing tricks. All of this was tempered by a great thirst for learning that is, in Latin and Greek.

Growing up close to the law, the young girl had the opportunity to read the *Revised Statutes of the State of New York* from her father's library. Naively, she marked every page in which she saw laws that curtailed women's rights and freedoms, with the intent of cutting them out of the book and out of existence. With her expanding interest in the world, at age sixteen she was already enrolled in the Troy Female Seminary. It was the same college to which both Lucy and Susan had applied without managing to obtain a scholarship. In the school, in addition to the expected embroidery, music, and dancing, she also explored math, history, and classical languages (she learned Greek). She enjoyed all subjects except religion. Her encounter with that came in a dramatic fashion with the Second Great Awakening and its most famous evangelist, Charles Finney. Elizabeth, strong in her self-independence, was one of the few students in the all-female school who was not converted. She had a conversation with Charles Finney himself, but the experience left her reeling with nightmares of hell and damnation, from which she recovered, thanks to the help of family trips to Niagara Falls.

When destiny placed charming Henry Brewster Stanton in her way, the eager student did not complete her studies. Stanton was an abolitionist lecturer, whom she first saw at the podium and whose words enthralled her. It was love at first sight and led to an engagement within weeks. The new wife soon discovered that Henry Stanton's views about the freedom of the African American did not extend to the home, where he was rather a traditionalist. Only in the beginning did Henry bend a little toward Elizabeth's sentiments, even though the marriage lasted past the golden anniversary.

Elizabeth discovered her oratorical talents on the first day in Seneca Falls when she rose to address the audience. By the end of the day, she was already a recognized leader of a new movement. The Declaration was mostly her work, and it was far from a repetition of Thomas Jefferson's Declaration, since nine tenths of it was original writing. Through the experience of Seneca Falls, Elizabeth became aware of her gifts as a leader and as an orator able to address a crowd extemporaneously. On the other hand, she was equally able to write and to report the proceedings.

Not only was Elizabeth a born leader and orator, but also a prolific writer for the cause. She knew how to use both well-crafted sentences and a humor that had bite. In the *Lily* (a temperance paper published in Seneca Falls by the Bloomers), she wrote pieces such as "Confessions of a Housekeeper," "The Model Wife," and "Woman's Rights and Woman's Wrongs According to the Law"; she also wrote popular pamphlets.

In 1842 Elizabeth's first child had been born. In a reversal of fate for the Cady lineage, she gave birth only to boys from the first four pregnancies; the first daughter was born ten years later. Elizabeth bore six of her seven children with great ease, a witness to her good health and vitality. All her children survived, strengthening in her the belief of her own exceptionalism. The daring innovator was an unconventional mother; she encouraged the development of personality even when it manifested in whims, and she enjoyed what looked like a spoiled brood.

She paid attention to exercise, the open air, and healthful food, wanting her children to be healthy, energetic, and self-reliant.

In spite of the pleasure it gave her, the time devoted to mothering also caused her distress because of its all-encompassing nature and the lack of marital support. She suffered from being closed off from the world and from the women's cause by her family. By the middle of the 1850s, her tasks lessened, and the pressure was eased when she hired a young helper, who stayed in the household for thirty years.

Susan B. Anthony called Elizabeth "my special sister."[5] They were friends for more than fifty years and shared the leadership of the movement. Their first collaboration took the form of setting up the women's conventions in the early 1850s; together they prepared speeches and meetings. In gratitude for her friend's untiring help, Elizabeth stated, "I forged the thunderbolts, she fired them."[6]

Susan B. Anthony: The Napoleon of the Movement

Born on February 15, 1820, in Adams, Massachusetts, Susan Brewster Anthony was the daughter of the strict but open-minded Quaker Daniel Anthony. He was devoted to humanitarian causes and harbored runaway slaves in his house. As a small child, Susan observed firsthand what slavery meant. Luminaries like Frederick Douglass, William Lloyd Garrison, and Wendell Phillips also visited the Anthony house.

When Susan was six, the family moved to Battenville, New York, where her father acquired a mill and operated the business quite successfully. Her father took part in her education for a time, especially after a teacher refused to teach her long division because of her gender. Susan's mother, Lucy, was not Quaker herself, but was supportive of her husband's ideas. She bore seven children in sixteen years, suffering depression and fragile health.

For a time at least, Susan was sent off to expensive Quaker boarding schools. However, the father's business went bankrupt in the depression of 1837, and in 1845 he moved his family to Rochester. At this point Susan was a governess, and she later taught at the Canajoharie Academy, east of Albany. There she joined the local chapter of the Daughters of Temperance, delivering her first public speech in March 1849.

Susan determined to set the course of her life independent of marriage, and she remained a committed single woman to her death. She feared, for good reason, that marriage would sidetrack her from her life task. Susan's militancy started with taking up the issue of temperance in order to protect women and children from the abuse of drunken heads of family. Later she promoted the antislavery movement, with a mind to stopping the abuse of black women by the slaveholders. She also championed some women's rights issues, such as married women's property acts and guardianship rights over children.

As was the case with Lucy Stone, one of Susan's early awakenings came from realizing that as a teacher, for an equal position, she received only two thirds of the wage of her male colleagues. Later her resolve took definite shape when she read Lucy Stone's speech, reprinted by Horace Greeley. At age thirty, she became a paid professional lecturer, promoting both abolition and women's rights. She faced the harassment and disruptions caused by men, insults that went as far as hanging her in effigy, clergymen refusing her access to their churches, empty halls and long travels, and the mockery of the newspapers. In 1871, she calculated that in that year alone, she had given 171 lectures and traveled some thirteen thousand miles. And this is what she did for many years thereafter.

In the temperance movement, Susan experienced anew the force of discrimination in 1853, when the representatives from the New York State Female Temperance Society were denied attendance at the World Temperance Convention. Together with William Lloyd Garrison, Lucy Stone, and Antoinette Brown, Susan organized later in the same year a "Whole World's Temperance Convention" in response to what they saw as a half-world's convention.

Susan appreciated Elizabeth Stanton's "big brain" as she called it, and Elizabeth, in turn, acknowledged the need to be awakened and spurred further along by her friend. Elizabeth summed up their relationship: "In thought and sympathy we were as one, and in the division of labor we exactly complemented each other. In writing we did better work than either could alone. While she is slow and analytic, I am rapid and synthetic. I am the better writer and she the better critic. She supplied the facts and the statistics, and I the philosophy and rhetoric."[7]

Elizabeth Cady Stanton and Susan B. Anthony: The Power of Two

Together the two women created the Women's Loyal National League before the end of the Civil War, and later the National Women Suffrage Association, with Elizabeth Stanton as its president and Susan B. Anthony as vice president. Susan became the legal owner of the short-lived weekly *The Revolution*, since Elizabeth, a married woman, could not own anything. However, most of the articles were penned by Elizabeth. She wrote about equal rights under the law; about the "single-sex standard"; about suffrage and equal pay for the same work; and also, more broadly, in favor of the eight-hour workday. Next door to the offices of *The Revolution*, Susan held the meetings of the Working Woman's Association. In effect, Susan was the legs and arms of an Elizabeth who was often homebound and tied to her family obligations.

The two women had a very dynamic friendship, rather than an acquiescing camaraderie or subservience on Susan's side. Over the span of fifty years, the two certainly had reason and opportunities to disagree and to part ways. Elizabeth acknowledged a debt of gratitude to Susan. "She has kept me on the warpath at the point of the bayonet so long … that before I was summoned, [I hoped] that I might spend the sunset of my life in some quiet chimney corner … Well, I prefer a tyrant of my own sex, so I shall not deny the patent fact of my subjection."[8]

To the optimism, passion, and abundance of forces of Elizabeth, Susan brought the counterweight of self-discipline, tireless devotion to the task, and self-reliance. In times when Elizabeth had to move away from the limelight, Susan tirelessly worked behind the scenes. While Elizabeth was engaged in public life, Susan always deferred to her and encouraged her leadership, even when others tried to promote Susan's own leadership. Even when in 1890, the two main women's associations, which had existed alongside each other for twenty years, merged to form the National American Woman Suffrage Association, Susan still fought to have her friend preside over it, and faithfully, Susan gave the second speech, after Elizabeth.

Throughout the years of their relationship, there were many occasions for disagreement. For example, during the time leading to the Civil War, Susan disagreed quite vocally with Elizabeth on discontinuing the women's fight and rallying to the antislavery movement. Later in life, Susan had to shake up her friend in moments of complacency, chief among them the occasion of the reunification of the two rival movements. And there were many other occasions to disagree over the years. For all their disagreements, the two never brought acrimony out in public, preferring to work it out between themselves, valuing the constructive challenge of the other. Even in jest, they could recognize each other's idiosyncrasies; Elizabeth condescendingly called her friend "poor Susan," and the other retorted "Queen Mother."[9]

At the end of their lives, the two were no longer as close. However, at Elizabeth's death in 1892, Susan went through a hard mourning, then followed her friend four years later. They died at almost the same age.

Launching the Women's Movement

From Seneca Falls and the Worcester Convention onward, women started to lecture widely, gaining confidence, strengthening friendships, creating issue-specific committees, filing petitions, writing letters and essays, raising money, editing newspapers, and resorting to acts of civil disobedience. They resisted forming an organization, hesitating to enter what they saw as men's form of operating, which had not served women in the past.

From 1848 until the Civil War began in 1861, the women held yearly conventions (except for 1857) in such places as Syracuse, Cincinnati, Cleveland, Philadelphia, Worcester, and New York City. The meetings continued to be civil. Even in 1858 when manifold contrasting concerns emerged (between radical thinkers, free-love advocates, and traditionalists), Lucretia Mott was there to uphold the Quaker openness to all concerns. Contrasts were even more pronounced in the 1860 convention, when Elizabeth Stanton offered a dozen resolutions on the matter of divorce, in which she was countered by Antoinette Brown Blackwell.

After the start of the Civil War, many of the leading personalities retired to private life for at least a good portion of their time. Such was the case for Elizabeth and the Grimke sisters; even Lucy Stone consciously decided to place a priority on her motherly duties. The unflagging Susan was left to hold the torch as the primary advocate for the cause.

Civil War and Internal Divisions

At the outbreak of the Civil War, women in the North dedicated themselves to supporting the war effort through charities and domestic projects.

Women activists placed their focus on the emancipation cause. And that was not an easy cause to support everywhere they went. During these years, Elizabeth and Susan formed the Woman's Loyal National League (WLNL), urging northern women to work for the suppression of slavery. They felt Lincoln was taking only very minimal and timid steps. The WLNL was born at a convention in New York City in 1863, and Elizabeth called it "the first and only organization of women for the declared purpose of influencing politics."[10] And so it was. The WLNL supported emancipation, and women's rights as well, although they were broadly and vaguely formulated. The first task of the growing organization was set at gathering a million signatures in a petition to end slavery. It was most likely Elizabeth's idea, but it was Susan who carried out the organizational piece, managing to enroll two thousand volunteers, who in turn collected approximately four hundred thousand signatures by the war's end.

Some of the differences among the women of the triumvirate were already appearing. Lucy, as an ardent antislavery militant, supported the WLNL; however, she disliked politics and refused to be an official lecturer. She started lecturing again at the war's end (1865), and together with Susan, she planned the next strategy, which included a petition drive for female suffrage.

Aftermath of the War

After the Civil War, women offered their messages by publishing and selling tracts and pamphlets, including the Seneca Falls "Declaration of Rights and Sentiments," "A Discourse on the Rights and Condition of Women" by Samuel May, letters by Elizabeth Stanton, and Harriot Hunt's "Protest against Taxation of Married Women."

Two issues of equality stood alongside and at odds with each other: the cause of the newly enfranchised black men and the cause of women. To the calls for patience and for giving priority to the Negro cause, Elizabeth responded with the December 1865 essay published in the *National Anti-Slavery Standard*, essentially asking for women's issues to be dealt with at the same time. She expressed that the idea that women should "stand aside and see 'Sambo' walk into the kingdom first" appalled her, further adding that a woman was far worse off with an uneducated free slave than with an educated white man.[11] These statements, shocking as they sound to modern consciousness, were far from rare and should be understood in light of the prejudices of the time. At bottom lay a deep-seated fear that the newly enfranchised block of voters would have more traditionalist views about the role of women, thus delaying women's rights. Such was also the fear of Lucretia Mott.

Growth of the Movement and Break

The eleventh national convention finally gathered in New York in May 1866. It saw the emergence of a new organization, the American Equal Rights Association (AERA); Lucretia was named its president, Elizabeth its vice president. The new Fourteenth Amendment to the Constitution repeated the word "male" three times, making it clear that women would not profit from what was going to be granted to black men.

During the years following the Civil War, Susan and Elizabeth made some questionable decisions; one of those was accepting the financial support of the extravagant, unreliable, and self-deluded philanthropist George F. Train. Although he was promoting the women's cause, he could at the same time utter the most racist comments. While Susan and Elizabeth fondly embraced his support, Lucy and her husband, Henry, were horrified, as was William Lloyd Garrison. All of them also questioned the wisdom of aligning themselves with the Democratic Party (Train was a Democrat). Lucretia was so dispirited by the choice that she considered withdrawing from all her AERA duties.

Later it was Victoria Woodhull who brought embarrassment to Elizabeth and Susan. Together with her sister Tennie, Victoria published *Woodhull and Claflin's Weekly*, which covered financial news, women's rights, and socialism. Added to this unusual mix was Victoria's advocacy for free love that predicated more than one sexual partner. Together with her magnetic personality, Victoria had the added strength of financial resources. A self-proclaimed seer, Victoria had married twice before becoming the protégé and favored companion of Cornelius Vanderbilt. With this leverage and influence, Victoria managed to speak in front of the House Judiciary Committee, arguing for a woman's right to vote. The National Woman Suffrage Association, which had just been formed by Elizabeth and Susan, offered its immediate support for the brazen adventurer. Woodhull went further, founding the People's Party and staging a presidential candidacy. Elizabeth took far too long to distance herself from the adventuresome courtesan, even after Susan had already become alarmed by the situation.

In 1868, Lucretia had resigned from the AERA while the debate over priority of female suffrage over black male suffrage was still very divisive. Things continued in the same mood the next year, when Congress passed the Fifteenth Amendment, which said that no state could deny the vote based on race. Elizabeth and Susan opposed the amendment for not going far enough, while Lucy supported it. At the request of others, Susan and Elizabeth resigned from their leadership of the AERA. Just two days later, they formed the NWSA (National Woman Suffrage Association). In doing so, they had not cared to invite Lucy and her husband, Henry, nor others in the movement. It was not too surprising, therefore, given this and other events, that in the fall of the same year, Lucy and Henry decided to go their own way and form the American Women Suffrage Association (AWSA). The AWSA was inaugurated much more formally than the NWSA, with careful preparations and invitations. The first convention in 1869 was attended by delegates from twenty-one states of the thirty-seven states existing at that time. Susan was present, inviting an atmosphere of tolerance between the two organizations; Elizabeth had far less tolerance and understanding.

The differences between the AWSA and NWSA may seem minimal in retrospect. As was just mentioned, the members of AWSA supported passage of the Fifteenth Amendment; not so the NWSA. The first focused on suffrage at the state level; the NWSA's strategy of choice was the ratification of a new constitutional amendment. The AWSA allowed for both male and female members and officers; at its incipience, only female members were allowed in NWSA. The AWSA had a strict focus on suffrage; its counterpart took on additional challenges, such as divorce law and married women's property rights. These differences are not surprising, given Elizabeth's wide range of interests. The divisions between the two groups stemmed only in part from a clash of personalities; a greater part of the problem was an inability to forgive past hurts.

Meanwhile in the new territories of the West, something started to change. Wyoming was the first to accord suffrage to the ladies in 1869. The territory had a very small population of only nine thousand, and women stood in a ratio of one to six men. Granting the vote to women was a way to encourage them to come from the East. Utah became the second territory to extend suffrage, doing so in the hope of dampening opposition to Mormon polygamy. In the states, nothing of the sort had happened yet.

Toward Reunification and Success

The road toward women's suffrage was paved with more and more direct actions and symbolic events. In 1872 in Rochester, Susan and fourteen supporters cast their votes at a local election. Later Susan was brought to trial for this act. Having mounted a very efficient bully pulpit through a biting self-defense, Susan refused to pay the fine, opting for prison instead. Authorities thought it wise to ignore the fine, but Susan had received the attention she desired. In the same year, Elizabeth went to the poll claiming her right to vote.

On the centennial of the Boston Tea Party, commemorated on December 15, 1873, three hundred women supporters gathered in Faneuil Hall in Boston for a "New England Women's Tea Party," highlighting the similarity of women's position with that of the colonists before them. A similar celebration took place in Philadelphia. At the 1876 Philadelphia Centennial Exhibition, the women had their own pavilion, covering almost two-thirds of an acre. Lucy, more reserved and conservative than Susan and Elizabeth, had initially resisted involvement. Elizabeth drafted another "Declaration of Rights and Sentiments," and a dozen women signed it, including Lucretia Mott. On her side, Susan completed the staging of events. Having been refused an opportunity to address the public on the Fourth of July, she decided to take a stand. After the Declaration of Independence was read, Susan spread leaflets of the women's own Declaration to the surprised audience.

By now Elizabeth had become a very sought-after professional lecturer; from 1869 to 1879, she spent an average of eight months a year away from home with very lucrative engagements, and two agencies vied for her attention. She was a celebrity, and she enjoyed it. At this point in her life, she admitted her past mistakes, looking at them with distance and commenting, "For over thirty years some people have said from time to time that I have injured the suffrage movement beyond redemption; but it still lives. Train killed it, Victoria Woodhull killed it, *The Revolution* killed it. But with each death it put on a new life."[12]

Behind the scenes, more and more women were understanding the need to heal old wounds. Alice Blackwell, Lucy Stone's daughter, started playing an important role by editing the *Woman's Journal,* working at bridging the gap between AWSA and NWSA. In November 1872, Elizabeth's daughter Harriot approached Lucy and Alice in Dorchester, Massachusetts, and together they had an amiable time, but nothing fruitful ensued. The thirtieth anniversary celebration of Seneca Falls, held in Rochester in 1878, was one of the last events that Lucretia Mott could attend. She died two years later, and Elizabeth, delivering the eulogy, called her "the most remarkable woman of her time."[13] What stayed in everyone's memory was the fact that Mott never pronounced judgments or stinging rebukes. And she stood above the parties, doing all she could for their reunion. One could say this reconciling attitude continued to play an influence after her passing.

The tensions between NWSA and AWSA started to abate. NWSA's policy had become less divisive, partly because Elizabeth was spending much time in the United Kingdom and NWSA leaders accepted the success of the AWSA as instrumental to their movement. The younger generation was not invested in the personal feuds among the leaders. And in 1887, Lucy herself returned to working out ideas for healing the old rift. That winter Susan wrote to Lucy asking to discuss a plan for reunification. Susan, Lucy, Blackwell, and Rachel Foster met on December 31, 1887. Although Lucy still held grudges against Susan, which she expressed privately, the meeting represented a step forward.

The 1888 Women's Convention became a weeklong celebration of the fortieth anniversary of Seneca Falls and a first International Council of Women. Elizabeth would have failed to come if it had not been for a stinging letter of rebuke sent by Susan. Legend has it that Susan forced her to prepare a speech. The convention was truly international, with some eighty speakers from around the world. A picture of Lucretia Mott hung above the stage, and Elizabeth rightly invoked her benediction and her spirit. Still, the question of reunification had not emerged fully, and Alice Blackwell was feeling discouraged, fearing that her mother was not fully honored by the two other women. Fears notwithstanding, two months later, a document emerged, signed by the full triumvirate plus a host of other activists (among them Julia Ward Howe, Mathilda Joslin Gage, and Frances Willard), and titled "Open Letter to the Women of America." Lucy Stone offered to underwrite a national convention to merge the two organizations and thus create the hybrid NAWSA acronym. In February 1890, after a great celebration of Susan's seventieth birthday, on the first day of the convention, the two organizations were formally merged. As usual, Elizabeth was elected president and Susan vice president, while Lucy took the chair of the executive committee. It was clear that Elizabeth, who was constantly traveling and lecturing, would hardly exercise her function; this left Susan as de facto president.

A Solitude of Self

The NAWSA's focus became the passing of a constitutional amendment. In 1878 Elizabeth was invited to speak to Congress, but only to a skeptical committee and with little success. In 1886 the women's agenda moved one step further and reached the Senate, thanks in large part to the signatures gathered by Frances Willard's Woman's Christian Temperance Union's petition endorsing an amendment for woman suffrage (the "Susan B. Anthony Amendment"); it gathered two hundred thousand signatures. The following year the Senate voted on the amendment for the first time, but, quite predictably, defeated it.

The amendment was routinely brought to Congress for reconsideration year after year until 1897, and then it disappeared for a time, until 1913.

With the growing exposure, progress started occurring elsewhere: women were allowed to vote in municipal elections in Kansas, and in the same state a woman mayor was elected in Oskaloosa. Great progress was made in higher education; women's college enrollment was now 35 percent of the nation's total. Women started entering white-collar professions as stenographers and typists; they also began to work in the department stores and federal and state offices. Progress was much slower in the legal profession.

In 1891 Lucy and Elizabeth testified together before the House Committee on the Judiciary. Elizabeth returned to the Judiciary Committee the following year, presenting her written essay "Solitude of Self," which was also read at her final NAWSA convention.[14] She began this famous address by saying that everything relevant had already been said at Committees of the Judiciary for the previous twenty years and that "the point I wish to bring plainly before you on this occasion is the individuality of each human soul"—perhaps an unusual introduction to the matter. And it was individuality that she addressed all through the essay: "the solitude and personal responsibility of her own individual life the birthright to self-sovereignty ... the immeasurable solitude of self." It is around individuality that Elizabeth's whole argument was built, an individuality that does not differentiate man from woman.

Elizabeth built a case, most convincingly, that woman cannot be denied the right to vote when she is already contributing as equal to man in art, science, literature, and civil matters. She repeated the same for education: "In talking about education, how shallow the argument that each class must be educated for the special work it proposed to do; and all those faculties not needed in that special walk must lie dormant and utterly wither for want of use; when perhaps, these will be the very faculties needed in life's greatest emergencies." And she concluded, "Who, I ask you, can take, dare take, on himself the rights, the duties, the responsibilities of another human soul?"

Surprisingly, the piece did not please Susan, but it delighted Lucy Stone, who reprinted it in full in her *Woman's Journal*. The two extremes of the women's movement had come closer in spirit. In "Solitude of Self,"

Elizabeth's radicalism was distilled to a radicalism of the spirit. That could only please Lucy, who found no fault in religion itself, but only in the interpretation made by the clergy. "Solitude of Self" had the stamp of an Emersonian self-reliance applied to the condition of women. In effect, Elizabeth was asking that women be allowed to be as self-reliant as men when facing all the challenges of life, that women abandon the idea that somehow their lot should be made easier by relying on men, and that men stop cultivating the illusion that they can make the task easier for women.

Reaching the Goal

Lucy Stone's presence in Chicago in May 1893 at the World's Congress of Representative Women was one of her last public appearances. The speech she had prepared (one of the few to find its way into print) was entitled "The Progress of Fifty Years."

Lucy Stone was already suffering from advanced stomach cancer and had written final letters to friends and relatives. Quite prepared for the event, she died in October of the same year, at age seventy-five. In death as in life, she established a precedent. According to her wishes, her body was cremated, making her the first person in Massachusetts to do so.

Elizabeth could not resist using her sharp tongue or witty penmanship to stir controversy, even in later life. She admitted, "I have always been in a chronic condition of rebellion."[15] This is why she criticized the clergy and religion, emphasizing that the churches had been woman's strongest enemy. She blamed the clergy's literal interpretation of the Bible. Early in life she had decided to write a criticism of the Bible, but nearly all her friends declined to help her. She had to put the project on hold until the years 1886 to 1895. She passed away in 1902, at the age of eighty-seven.

Susan served as president of NAWSA from 1892 to 1900, but she attended her last NAWSA convention in 1895. She carried a deep grief at Elizabeth's passing; her own passage to the other side was in 1906, only four years after her devoted friend. Eventually the Nineteenth Amendment to the US Constitution would be passed in 1920, and it would be called the Susan B. Anthony Amendment.

In 1897 New York State became the first and only state in the East to give women the right to vote before the passage of the Nineteenth Amendment twenty-three years later. Another fifteen states (mostly in the West) gave women the right to vote before the Susan B. Anthony Amendment became the law of the land. Although the inspiration for woman suffrage had come initially from America, by the time the Nineteenth Amendment passed in the United States, Austria, the Netherlands, Canada, New Zealand, and Australia had already given women the right to vote.

Elizabeth Cady Stanton and Susan B. Anthony formed a duality on the one hand; the two of them were balanced out by Lucy Stone on the other hand. Although many women played a variety of important roles in passing the Nineteenth Amendment, that outcome would have happened without their key contributions. We have seen how Cady Stanton stood as the ideologue, the source of inspiration and ideas, and Anthony complemented her with a complete devotion to the cause and relentless activity. While the first one was at times inconstant, the second kept her eyes on the prize without wavering. Another polarity within the movement appeared between AWSA (Lucy Stone) and its more radical counterpart of NWSA (Cady Stanton and Anthony). Lucy's approach was more gradual and less radical. Although she could not gain the appeal and aura of Elizabeth, she was the one who published the *Woman's Journal* for a far longer time than Elizabeth's and Susan's *Revolution*. Although Lucy lacked the desire to take front stage and assume risks, some of the radical steps taken (especially by Elizabeth) turned out to be a liability for the whole movement. AWSA and NSWA offered complementarity to each other; their reunion in NAWSA assured true strength for the whole movement.

Women's rights are but the tip of the iceberg of a larger phenomenon in the whole of Western civilization. The archetypal feminine has been revered since time immemorial in all traditions and all religions. The feminine had been obscured in Christianity, although not in its deeper traditions. All Christian denominations had lost sight of the feminine aspect of divinity; hence the patriarchal aspect of all Western societies and the degradation of individual women. Women's suffrage, and the celebration of Mother's Day or Women's Day, marked only the beginning of a long-overdue reintegration of societal values.

Women's rights were an important milestone in extending the notion "that all [human beings] are created equal." It may be surprising now to see the acrimony that once divided the issue of equality between African Americans and women. But many other issues in the realm of equality have come to the fore since the 1920s, of which no one would have had an inkling then. Suffice it to think about the rights of people with disabilities or of the gay rights movement to put things in perspective. The issue of equality will not be settled once and for all; it will simply keep growing with human consciousness.

Chapter 7

Earth Day: The Quest for Global Solidarity

I think there are good reasons for suggesting that the modern age has ended. Today many things indicate that we are going through a transitional period, when it seems that something is on the way out and something else is painfully being born. It is as if something were crumbling, and exhausting itself—while something else, still indistinct, is rising from the rubble.

—Vaclav Havel

The national holiday of Thanksgiving has consecrated the relationships of all ordinary citizens to their country and to each other. It is a festival of relationship, of belonging, which validates the contributions coming from the whole array of ethnicities, religions, and philosophies that form the tapestry of America. Last but not least, it unites us in the celebration of the bounties of the earth. This longing has been taken a step further in a new, evolving celebration, which is a gift of the United States to the world.

The Birth of a Global Holiday

Many people had a hand in what has now become Earth Day. Generally it is recognized that Senator Gaylord Nelson had the greatest individual impact on the genesis of the new holiday. But he was not the first nor the last; many others contributed important pieces to an observance that is still evolving.

March 21 or April 22: Complementary Meanings

Earth Day can be associated with two key individuals. The name and concept of Earth Day were allegedly pioneered by John McConnell at the 1969 UNESCO Conference on the Environment, held in San Francisco.[1] Earth Day was first observed the following year. McConnell's choice of date was March 21, the day of the spring equinox, a date of great significance for the planet. The first celebrations were held on March 21, 1970, in San Francisco, Davis, California, and possibly other cities. On that occasion, an Earth Day Proclamation was read by mayor Joseph Alioto in San Francisco. U Thant, secretary general of the United Nations, supported the initiative by reading his own declaration for the purpose.

About the same time, Wisconsin Senator Gaylord Nelson had called for a different kind of Earth Day, an environmental teach-in day that was first held on April 22, 1970.[2] Nelson announced his idea for a nationwide teach-in day on the environment in a speech to a conservation group in Seattle on September 20, 1969, and then again six days later in Atlantic City to a meeting of the United Auto Workers. In this way he brought the issue of the environment to conservationists and labor movement alike; this approach was already the first of a kind. Nelson had been moved to take action after witnessing the ravages of the 1969 oil spill in Santa Barbara, California. He felt outrage at the inertia of the political class and wanted the day to be the opportunity for basic education. More than twenty million people responded to his call during the first year. This second holiday expanded from being a national holiday to an international one around 1990.

The two different observances for our planet are complementary. One approach has a more spiritual tone—the recognition of earth/Gaia as a living being, from the Christian and spiritually oriented McConnell. A more activist approach came from the politician Nelson. Where the two overlap is in the educational dimension. To this day, the two aspects continue to go alongside each other, forming important complementary approaches.

The choice of March 21 was a significant way to honor the earth as a living being, since it marks an important day in the yearly earthly rhythms. All of this was in keeping with John McConnell's personality.

He was a child of the spring equinox, born on March 22, 1915, in Iowa. His interest in ecology awakened in 1939 while he was working in a plastics factory. At that early stage, he realized the impact that plastic manufacturing would have on the planet. Alongside ecology, he developed concern about pacifism. Since 1963 for the next seven years, McConnell worked on his "Minute for Peace" campaign. He launched it with a broadcast on December 22, 1963, the day that ended the mourning period for President Kennedy's death.

A practicing Christian, McConnell believed human beings have an obligation to steward the earth and its resources responsibly. The first picture of the earth from space moved him to design and create what later became the well-known earth flag. This image led him in 1969 to propose a holiday that would uphold the earth's beauty and sacredness. To the earth flag was added an "Earth Day Anthem," set to Beethoven's "Ode to Joy" melody.

The April 22 Earth Day was much more prosaic a choice than its March 21 counterpart. Nelson chose the date to maximize participation on college campuses. He wanted to avoid exams, spring breaks, and conflict with religious holidays of the spring, while still having warm weather. He wanted a time when students would be in class, and so he initially chose a Wednesday.

The Power of Networks

Denis Hayes, another Wisconsinite, read about the projected Earth Day in a *New York Times* article when he was a Harvard graduate student.[3] Though born in Wisconsin in 1944, Hayes was raised mainly in Camas, Washington. At Stanford University, where he received his undergraduate degree in history, everything prepared him for the life of a visionary. There he had been president of the student body and an activist against the Vietnam War. Then he enrolled at Harvard's Kennedy School of Government. Organizing Boston's Earth Day would have been enough for him; however, Senator Nelson had bigger plans for Hayes: selecting a staff and coordinating the Earth Day effort nationwide. Eventually Hayes did just that and dropped his Harvard studies.

Hayes put full trust in young college graduates. Together, they managed to pull off the difficult task of coordinating autonomous organizations that were very loosely networked. From this first success, Hayes went on to found the Earth Day Network, and with it he reached approximately 180 nations, making this the world's most widely observed secular holiday.

In addition to promoting the holiday, the Earth Day Network supported other forms of environmental activism, like global policies, public environmental campaigns, and coordinated actions. Earth Day Network members include nonprofits, local governments, and activists. Internationally the network includes some twenty thousand organizations in more than 190 countries, coordinating countless efforts of environmental protection and community development.

Nelson launched his Earth Day with an attempt to unite conservation and labor concerns, trying to enlarge the movement for the environment beyond traditional constituencies. Thus it was normal that he would reach out to Republican Representative Pete McCloskey, to whom he offered a role as cochair in a new nonprofit organization, Environmental Teach-In, Inc., to get the initiative off the ground. Both Nelson and McCloskey campaigned for the event in the months to follow.

Pete McCloskey was born on September 29, 1927, in Loma Linda, California. Like Hayes, he was a graduate of Stanford University.[4] He received his undergraduate degree from Stanford in 1950 and graduated from Stanford University Law School in 1953. Quite unlike his colleagues in the ecological movement, before his studies, McCloskey had enlisted voluntarily in the US Marine Corps from 1945 to 1947 and the US Marine Corps Reserve for another eight years. He retired from the Reserve in 1974.

McCloskey was elected as a Republican to the House of Representatives in 1967 and was reelected continuously until 1983. Despite his military career, he was probably the first Republican to oppose the Vietnam War. He even sought the 1972 Republican presidential nomination on a specifically anti-Vietnam War platform against incumbent President Richard Nixon, but was, predictably, defeated. Consistently, he also opposed the Iraq War in 2003.

It is estimated that the first April 22, 1970, Earth Day included participation by two thousand colleges and universities, some ten thousand primary and secondary schools, and numerous cities and communities nationwide, involving an estimated twenty million Americans, peacefully invoking environmental legislation. The grassroots dimension of the event had been its strength and determining factor.

Twenty years later, participation in the event reached the number of two hundred million people in some 140 countries. The significance of Earth Day activities in 1990 created a sizable impact on the recycling policies of many countries and mobilized the energies for a United Nations Earth Summit, held in Rio de Janeiro in 1992.

Earth Day 2000 extended the dimension of international activism thanks to the worldwide web. An estimated 184 countries involved more than five thousand environmental groups beyond the United States, reaching hundreds of millions. Earth Day is clearly here to stay. What was started with Earth Day continues to this day in a yearning for bringing together the two streams: science with social activism, brought together with a spirituality that recognizes the living dimension of the earth.

A Blend of Spirit and Politics

A young woman with no past affiliations with political or ecological movements has become a symbol embodying the striving to blend diverse social concerns, to practice a new brand of social activism— one that sees spirit as being integral to, rather than separate from, the struggle for respect of Mother Earth and of our brothers and sisters. She is one of many examples.

An Earth Day High above the Ground

Just before Earth Day 1999, a group of striking metalworkers from Washington State hiked all the way to a mountain in Humboldt County, California, to the tree that a woman of great determination had been inhabiting (or more precisely, tree sitting) for more than a year; that was how long she had stayed on a platform built on a redwood tree. Through her convictions and persistence, even without a premeditated plan, she had managed to bring together two related issues: labor and protection of the environment. David Foster, a leader of the United Steelworkers of America, had come all the way from Washington State to honor personally the one who had been a continuous source of inspiration for the striking steelworkers. Foster was determined to climb the tree on his own. Actually, he needed the help of a pulley system to make it up to the platform the woman occupied.

Though brief, their encounter was a significant one. Two movements had reached out to each other, and the inspired action of a woman had played a great role in this achievement. Big, burly, reputedly tough guys could look up to a young, slender, spontaneous woman, who had strengthened her resolve and undergone a transformational initiation high in the branches of one of the most ancient trees in America. This was the prelude to Earth Day proper. The next event would be a women's affair; it was the surprise visit of singers Joan Baez and Bonnie Raitt. With the newly devised pulley system, the two musicians made it up the tree. At first the three were alone, and then two filmmakers came up. They had a conversation, then the artists sang, and the younger woman shared her poems.

A Tree and a Tree Dweller

The young woman living on a platform in the thousand-year-old redwood tree named Luna was Julia Butterfly Hill; she stayed there 738 days between December 1997 and December 1999, celebrating there both her twenty-fourth and twenty-fifth birthdays. Her odyssey is retold in *The Legacy of Luna: The Story of a Tree, a Woman, and the Struggle to Save the Redwoods.*[5] During that time, Julia never descended or touched the ground, learning to negotiate life high up on a platform on which she could not even stand straight. Only in December 1998 did she move partway down the trunk to a much sturdier and wider platform.

Julia Butterfly Hill's connection with the environmental cause was already in place before she knew it. While growing up, she had traveled extensively with her family and often explored rivers close to the campgrounds. At age six, while she was taking a hike with her family, a butterfly alighted on her finger, accompanying her for the whole hike. That was the origin of her nickname, Butterfly.

But a connection with nature is hardly sufficient in itself to prepare a young woman for the formidable constraints of life up high in one of the highest trees of creation, where tight space, lack of amenities, solitude, and weather extremes could break any soul. Julia's path had been laid in the first ten years of her life, ever since her father, a traveling preacher, had taken his family with him from town to town in a thirty-two-foot camper. The child shared that small, contained space with her father, mother, and two younger brothers.

When she was ten, the family settled in Jonesboro, Arkansas. Her life became the normal life of a teenager, with hardly any other expectations than the usual. Among these, she had the desire to strike out and reach success and directed her intentions toward business school. But at age twenty-two, something else was in store for the young woman. In August 1996 she was driving for a friend who had been drinking, when the car was hit from behind by a drunken driver in what came to be a near-fatal crash. The steering wheel jammed her right eye into her skull. To recover, she had to go through long months of intensive therapy that helped her retrieve short-term memory and motor skills. It took much longer than that to look at her life and see herself in a different light. "I also saw that had I not come through the way I did, I would have been very disappointed with my empty life.... I resolved to change my life, and I wanted to follow a more spiritual life."[6] On coming out of therapy, she embraced the idea of traveling around the world. She never made it past California's Humboldt County.

A stranger had mentioned the redwoods along the Lost Coast to Julia's traveling party. Julia found herself very eager to visit Grizzly State Park and see the ancient trees for the first time. "As I crossed the highway, I felt something calling to me. Upon entering the forest, I started walking faster, and then, feeling this exhilarating energy, I broke into a run, leaping over logs as I plunged in deeper."[7] (Unknowingly, she had just walked next to the property of Pacific Lumber/Maxxam Corporation, owned by Texan tycoon Charles Hurwitz. Not far behind the screen of the old forest lay the path of destruction that Charles

Hurwitz had ordered his newly acquired Pacific Lumber to make in the name of short-term profit. Witnessing this as she walked out of the forest, Julia felt like a different woman. Moved by the power of the moment, she decided to pray for guidance and chose a special spot between some trees and a stream. After the prayer, it was easier to forgo the world journey she had been dreaming of; she felt very serene about an activist choice that would be anything but easy.

She went back home and sold her belongings in order to finance her next step. "[A] deep and compelling sense told me that I had to walk the path I had chosen; or rather, the path that seemed to have chosen me. There was a calling and I would not be at peace until I fulfilled it"[8] In Arcata, California, she called the Environmental Protection and Information Center (EPIC), and they directed her to a base camp where direct action was organized. When she arrived at the base camp, she realized it was being closed down, and she felt quite disappointed. Seeking something else to do, she decided to go to Eureka, seven miles to the south, where a rally was being held.

A speaker addressed the crowd, informing them about police brutality, and then invited others to the microphone. Knowing little about the issue, Julia nevertheless felt compelled to speak. All she knew was what she had seen—forests being destroyed. The passion in her plea claimed the attention of a certain Shakespeare (nom de guerre), who felt Julia was the kind of person he could work with. That was fortunate; at that point, Shakespeare was the only one who had noticed Julia's desire, and the coming winter was drawing direct action to a lull. In the following days, she found herself waiting to see what she was called to do, with only Shakespeare encouraging her to hang on. Finally, one day an activist asked for a volunteer to "sit in Luna," and Julia found herself answering positively and with enthusiasm, even if with little precise understanding. On his side, the activist accepted her offer only because there were no other volunteers.

Climbing the steep slope to the tree already was an ordeal for Julia, who ran out of breath and then started to experience self-doubt. Her first tree-sit under the rain was the next trial; the cotton clothes she was wearing stayed wet and cold. The tree was called "Luna" (Spanish for moon) because the platform on top of it had been built by the light of the full moon. Earth First had established Luna as a site for tree-sitting; Julia was not affiliated with that organization. And at that moment, she still had scanty education about sustainable forestry or environmental matters.

Luna is a unique tree in a unique location. The ancient redwood stands atop a cliff, where it is exposed to high winds and lightning, and in the past, to forest fires. At its bottom are two "caves," with charred linings that extend almost completely through the trunk. The lower branches have completely broken off, and many burls cover the trunk throughout. Not far from the top is another cave, the result of a lightning fire. Nor does the charm and uniqueness of Luna diminish on its upper half. In Julia's words, "There's a whole forest in her, and it's absolutely magical. Ferns, salmonberry, and huckleberry grow in Luna's pockets where duff has collected over the years. There are many different fungi and mosses and lichens; *usnia* hangs down like Spanish moss; scalloped, whitish gray lichen and teeny, tiny mushrooms shaped like satellite dishes nestle in her folds; green, furry moss, dark in the center and neon at its edges, coats her sides. Especially in the fog, Luna is a fairy tale waiting to happen."[9]

Julia's first trial by fire was climbing the tree with only a minimal, on-the-spot crash course in climbing. On the platform she met with two other occupiers and spent the first sleepless, windy, and stormy nights, coming down on the sixth day. The very next day, she was asked whether she wanted to go back up to replace the two male occupants, and she immediately felt called to do so. This second time she was better prepared to face the weather, but she got very sick, with accompanying extreme hot and cold flashes and convulsions. It was around Thanksgiving time, and she left the tree when relief arrived, later discovering that she had been suffering from two viruses, one of which had moved into her kidneys. At this point, Luna was under attack; the next harvest plan by Pacific Lumber included that tree.

The New Economic Challenge to Planet Earth

Winter was approaching, and most of the activists would be leaving. There was not going to be anyone to safeguard Luna. Julia had gone up the tree with a certain activist named Almond. Pacific Lumber, who owned the land, started cutting the side shoots from the base of Luna, then the trees around it, and finally a big Douglas fir just next to Luna. The cutting went on until December 23. Witnessing destruction and desolation all around her, Julia felt how strongly hate within herself directed her to strike back in pain. Hate became even hate for herself, for being part of the race that was degrading the earth beyond its tipping point. She felt the need to pray. "I knew that if I didn't find a way to deal with my anger and hate, they would overwhelm me and I would be swallowed up in the fear, sadness, and frustration."[10] She realized through prayer that it is the love of creation that gives us life and sustains us no matter what we do as human beings. The destructive forces set loose upon the environment by the likes of Hurwitz can end up sapping the strength of the most determined activists; by hating, they hollow themselves out and burn out.

Julia's companion could not accompany her through this ordeal of soul, and soon he had to leave the tree. She now knew from within herself that activism alone would not suffice to hold on for the long term. And she knew that she needed to reach beyond stereotypes in order to affect the world of the loggers. This was the theme of many months to follow: dying to the old self each time a new task or a new challenge would arise. On the other side stood the forces of Charles Hurwitz and Maxxam, who knew better than anyone else how to test every fiber of human nature, with no remorse for doing so.

Charles Hurwitz had leveraged the buyout of a sound and sustainable business, Pacific Lumber, which had a large amount of assets. Hurwitz had a flair for buying businesses with undervalued stock and then liquidating their assets. He had leveraged the buyout of Pacific Lumber with the help of high-interest junk bonds devised by notorious white-collar criminals such as Michael Milken and Ivan Boesky (who was later sent to jail for insider trading). But to do that buyout, Hurwitz incurred a hefty debt of $800 million; hence the need to sell off the company's assets fast and to clear-cut the forest for quick returns.

Because of the Endangered Species Act, which Congressman Pete McCloskey had coauthored in 1973, Pacific Lumber actually did not have the right to log the area. Ignoring that, however, the federal government and the state of California had offered to pay some $480 million to obtain not only the Headwaters Forest Agreement, but also to buy land already logged by Pacific Lumber. The Headwaters Forest Agreement proposed to save 3,500 acres of ancient redwood forest, while sacrificing thousands of other acres of old-growth forest. Further, the action was ignoring the fact that Maxxam had already been accused of looting a savings and loan association (United Savings of Texas), whose bailout had cost US taxpayers some $1.6 billion. There was little or nothing that Hurwitz was willing to concede. In exchange for the profitable deal, Pacific Lumber had offered a sustainable yield plan that was sustainable only in name and that did not speak of any measures of restoration. Years later, evidence emerged that the plan had been fraudulent.

In fact, Pacific Lumber under Hurwitz had doubled or tripled the rate of cutting to maximize profits. The real plan was to extract everything possible from the land within twenty years, then lay off all the employees. By leaving a few trees in the area, Pacific Lumber was technically avoiding clear-cutting. They followed this sham with dumping diesel fuel and napalm, lighting a fire, and killing even the few leftover trees. This practice is, in fact, reminiscent of the napalm burning in Vietnam. After having savagely depleted the soil and causing massive landslides in places, the company then added chemical fertilizers. After the destruction, two trees were planted for every one cut down, replacing the original diversity with a monoculture everywhere in sight.

Under Hurwitz, Pacific Lumber had been cited by the California Department of Forestry more than three hundred times for violating the California State Forest Practices Act. Among those violations were destroying critical habitats, threatening endangered species, destroying air and water quality, and creating the conditions for massive landslides—and all of these were considered "minor" by the Department of Forestry. One example from among the many: logging an old Douglas fir stand in the locality known as Mattole, an area sacrificed in the Headwaters deal. It is an area of high seismic activity in which three faults intersect. It is highly prone to earthquakes and furthermore is part of an area with the highest rainfall in California. These are all factors for predicting landslides. None of this seemed to present a problem for the California

Department of Forestry, but neither did previous logging in the Stafford area, where a landslide had buried the homes of seven families.

These examples portray the new kind of entrepreneurship sanctioned by political fiat. This is Hurwitz in California. A look at Hurwitz in Washington State is just as illuminating. Following a familiar scheme, Hurwitz bought the family-owned Kaiser Aluminum, once again using junk bonds. And once again, to wipe off the debt, he had to suck the company dry. In the 1990s the workers were asked to take a wage cut because steel prices had decreased, and they were told their wages would be restored. After prices rose again and Maxxam netted a very large profit, the workers claimed restoration of their wages. But things remained the same for the workers, who were making two dollars an hour less than colleagues in the area; Maxxam workers were covered with fewer benefits as well. Maxxam refused to hear these or any other complaints. When the workers went on strike, the company locked them out and denied them employee status, hiring scab workers in their stead. Sometime later, these two issues, those of Pacific Lumber and of Kaiser Aluminum, environment and labor, would be brought together at the base of a tree.

Standing the Ground

Pacific Lumber explored more than one option to dislodge Julia. At first there was a campaign of intimidation, with a helicopter flying up close to the tree, hovering right overhead. After the event was reported to the Federal Aviation Administration, Pacific Lumber was not allowed to hover close to the tree or harvest the timber in its proximity. (Incidentally, the activist group Earth First decided, as well, that Julia had to leave the tree; many in the movement saw it as a rogue tree sit-in, defying internal agreements, because Julia had not asked for permission.)

Having failed with the quick measures, Pacific Lumber tried to starve the unwelcome guest by placing security guards at the base of the tree in the middle of one of the coldest winters on record, an El Niño year. Cold alone had begun to be a formidable foe: Julia's feet were turning blue and purple because of frostbite. The excruciating pain eventually subsided and healed. In order to face cold and the possibility of hunger, Julia remembers praying "like I haven't prayed in a long, long time. I prayed to every power and every God."[11] Still, for a week she was hardly able to sleep, nor could she stop crying. The storms and the blockade were taking a toll on her. Below, however, the activists managed to bring her food by creating a diversion. Realizing that they could not ensure a state of siege, the company pulled the guards from the scene, partly because of the cold and partly because of the difficulty of blocking supplies.

The external tests alternated with inner trials for Julia. "Why am I staying here?… What am I really trying to achieve?" were questions in Julia's mind. Adapting to life in a tree was another trial, and that was much more than a matter of organization. It was something that required a new way of looking at things. One day, tossed by a storm while holding onto Luna and praying to her, Julia heard the tree calling to her: "Julia, think of the trees in the storm."[12] She realized that what the trees do was what she needed to do: let go, let flow; not just continue to be strong, but act like the trees, who let themselves be blown and tossed. "I let my muscles go. I let my jaw unlock. I let the wind blow and the craziness flow. I bent and flailed with it, just like the trees, which flail in the wind. I howled. I laughed. I whooped and cried and screamed and raged. I hollered and I jibbered and I jabbered."[13]

She feared for her sanity, but at the same time realized that this was the call to let go of all externalities, images of self, and public personas, in favor of a fuller way of being. "I was going to live my life guided from the higher source, the Creation source. I couldn't have realized any of this without having been broken emotionally and spiritually and mentally and physically…. I had to be broken until I saw no hope, until I went crazy, until I finally let go. Only then could I be rebuilt; only then could I be filled back up with who I am meant to be. Only then could I become my higher self. That's the message of the butterfly."[14]

Almost twenty years later, her childhood connection to nature acquired a new depth, the butterfly of her childhood, the meaning of her nickname. Like the caterpillar, she had to let go of the external comforts and find the inner strength to enclose herself in a cocoon. That is a stage of facing attachments, assumptions, and inner demons. Later the cocoon can become a safe world in itself; after that, going back to the real world, leaving the secure environment, becomes the next challenge.

The World's Response

From that point on, Julia's struggle took on new dimensions, and the world responded to her inner change. Leonard Peltier, a Lakota Sioux, and other individuals of the American Indian Movement (AIM) presented her with an award; also she received the *Wage Peace Recognition of Valor* by the Veterans for Peace. Not only was the world starting to answer; even her relationship with Luna changed. Julia learned new skills, trusting herself to move around Luna without the protection of a harness. Using senses other than her sight, she used her whole body and spread her entire weight over her hands and feet. She decided to explore the top of the tree, thus seeing new aspects of the tree and experiencing new wonder.

In February 1998, about the time of her twenty-fourth birthday, Julia was interviewed and written about by the *Los Angeles Times, Newsweek,* and *People,* and she realized she had turned into a spokesperson for the movement. But that meant she was also publicly vilified by shock jocks (radio disc jockeys). Here, she used her new strengths to gain peoples' trust and defuse their enmity. On April 5, she was interviewed by CNN, together with John Campbell, president of Pacific Lumber; Julia came out the clear winner of the debate. At that point she was also under a lot of pressure, feeling keenly the responsibility of representing the movement to the world. "Things began to get overwhelming. I decided to fast and pray. When you cleanse your body, you also cleanse yourself mentally and spiritually. So I fasted and prayed, because this tree-sit needed some divine intervention."[15]

On the fourth day of the fast, she was visited by Robert Parker, a river guide and forest activist with a lot of media experience, who came to her with a very clearly set intention to help her with outreach. This providential help gave Julia the extra boost she needed. At this point, Luna's platform had basic equipment like a tape recorder, a digital camera, a video camera, an emergency cell phone, a pager/answering machine, walkie-talkies, a sophisticated radio phone powered by solar panels connected to two motorcycle batteries, and a hand-powered radio.

Media exposure gave way to new celebrations. Mickey Hart, a former Grateful Dead musician, brought music, and a crowd of supporters came to celebrate a sustainable future at the base of the tree. Then it was the turn of actor Woody Harrelson to visit and spend a night in the tree. Celebrities and media attention made Julia keenly aware of the need to continue her education so that she could speak out against the Headwaters Forest Agreement that proposed to save 3,500 acres of ancient redwood forest at the expense of thousands of acres of old-growth forest.

Fresh Challenges

Another important turning point lay in store. In the place called Mattole, after a lawsuit was filed, Pacific Lumber attempted to get in and cut. When activists blocked access, the company used new recruits who had been trained for pain compliance tactics, a euphemism for pursuing and beating up the activists. A month later, an activist called Gypsy was killed due to the negligence of an angry logger who wanted to scare him. Gypsy was twenty-four. The government did not pursue any inquiry, and police in riot gear stormed the blockade. At the height of violence and rage all around her, Julia called her mother to pray with her. "Together we prayed for the healing and the love and the strength that it was going to take for many people to make it through what happened ... And we prayed that I might find the strength to dig down deep and rediscover the love I would need to share with others in the face of this anger and violence."[16]

Because of the increasing traffic on the tree and the stress that it generated, the idea arose of building a second platform, lower and more comfortable. This new wonder looked like "a covered wagon without wheels," adding much comfort to the older one, just in time before winter closed in. Julia could finally stand up, and being lower down on the tree, the new place was cooler in hot weather and both warmer and less windy in winter. The new winter came punctually with snow, sleet, and hail. Julia had been one year on the tree, and people came to celebrate the anniversary. A rally with celebration was held at the nearby Redway Community Center. Julia listened in to it and contributed a poem, accompanied by various musicians. A new opportunity for celebration arose with the lighting of twenty-five battery-powered beacons that had been donated; they were lit every night from the day of the winter solstice until after Christmas, creating high visibility for miles around. By that time people were gaining courage; thirty-seven Stafford residents took the courage to sue Pacific Lumber for the landslide it had caused that had buried their houses.

The inner tug-of-war continued in Julia's mind. Was it time to come down from Luna, or should she continue to carry the message? She decided to leave the matter to her intuition. But at this point, prayer was not offering any immediate answer. Still, she knew she had to listen to herself and not let people's voices sway her and dictate her choices. "I knew prayer had taken me to the Lost Coast; prayer is what guided me to the redwood forest; and prayer is what led me to this tree and up this tree. Prayer is what had given me the strength to continue all this time. And someday, prayer would help guide me down."[17]

A resolution, even if slow, was already on the way. Julia had started to talk once a month with John Campbell, executive director of Pacific Lumber, the same man that she had outclassed on a television debate. Eventually she took the step of inviting him to talk to her on-site; when she climbed to the top of Luna, he could speak to her from a clearing at a same elevation only two hundred feet away. The two exchanged gifts: a six-pack of Coke for Julia and a crystal from Mount Ida for John. Julia began asking for the preservation of Luna plus a buffer of two hundred feet around the tree to bring the sit-in to a close.

Yet more tests were on the way. Julia was to experience in person the cruel acts toward nature that companies like Pacific Lumber perform routinely and that political powers callously rubber-stamp. After the clear-cuts in the vicinity of Luna, Pacific Lumber followed the harvest by dumping diesel fuel and napalm and lighting a fire. Julia witnessed and smelled the burns for six days. Her nose dried and started bleeding, her throat burned, and she was choked by smoke. After the public event on Earth Day, John Campbell started to discuss with Julia a deal for Luna.

At this time, a continent away, future Nobel Prize winner Wangari

Maathai was holding a significant action for the Kenyan greenbelt movement. In solidarity with her, Julia and others came up with the idea of an Interdependence Day, celebrated on July 3. On that day, despite very short notice, people held prayer and music circles in the area and in various states. Finally, it seemed that Julia and John were reaching a deal. On her team, Julia had Tryphena Lewis, former Tree Foundation support coordinator, and Herb Schwartz, a mediator and lawyer. But suddenly Charles Hurwitz was back to his bag of tricks, stalling the deal, and John Campbell was not returning Julia's calls. Maybe this was another tactic to deflate morale. The winter was coming on again, and Julia did not know whether she could face a third one.

When John Goodman, a striking Kaiser Aluminum steelworker, began calling Pacific Lumber on Julia's behalf, negotiations restarted and continued for several months. Goodman contacted Jared Carter, the vice president of Pacific Lumber, and they began negotiations to bring the tree-sit to an end. Julia was focusing on a resolution that would allow both sides to win, knowing that she would have to make concessions. She resisted attempts to curtail her freedom of expression as a condition for the deal. Because of leaks to the press from John Campbell, Julia held a press conference that generated support through which she could exert pressure on Senator Dianne Feinstein. Senator Feinstein, in turn, called on Pacific Lumber/Maxxam to let go of unreasonable demands. On December 18, 1999, the deal was signed, and a few days later Julia descended after more than two years of life in the tree and walked on firm ground.

A New Thanksgiving for Mother Earth

Much of the world, if not its entirety, is represented in the United States of America because of immigration. The nature of the Thanksgiving holiday allows a great step in the direction of universality. It is a step toward the brotherhood of human beings, the commonwealth of the human. Already many centuries ago, through the resilience of the human spirit, a bridge between the races had been formed through remarkable individuals such as Squanto and Pocahontas. Formidable economic interests rose against them, which disregarded any consideration of human values. Through those economic forces came colonization, and in its wake, slavery arose in the South, leaving behind an inheritance of hatred that has never completely abated.

Because America has been challenged to integrate the concerns of all races, it is not a surprise that an additional dream has taken shape on our soil, the concern for earth herself. In typical American fashion, another holiday has emerged that has now assumed international proportions. Earth Day has been a variety of things for me: sometimes an event organized in an urban square with booths, nonprofits, education, vendors, music, addresses, and interfaith services. In other years, it was a day for community service, such as collecting litter from around the highways, and then getting together for a potluck dinner; in between, or after, maybe some readings and some songs. Or more soberly, it was a time to spend in a worldwide connection to pray for the earth, speak to each other by candlelight, and so forth. What remains through all of this is a growing awareness that links us all worldwide.

On the day of Thanksgiving, America can look inward and celebrate the little cosmos that our land has become. Originally, the holiday also celebrated the bounty of the products of the earth. On Earth Day, we can look outward and remind ourselves of the world at large, human and nonhuman; we can celebrate its life and beauty, the brotherhood of the human and the natural; we can spread resolve for the stewardship of our planet.

Between Hope and Self-Destruction

We live in an evolving social reality that is continuously eluding our intellectual understanding; it can be apprehended only from within, when we are part of it. It cannot be fully apprehended from a spectator consciousness. Everything around us continuously offers us the most obvious aspects of this spectator consciousness: degradation, dissolution, emptiness, disintegration; we could call it the crumbling of everything that comes from the past. The monopolies of colonial times, which made America an economic colony, have now spread worldwide from America as their center. What formerly was a cause of human degradation now affects the entire globe itself. The only stakeholders that this sort of globalization recognizes are shareholders. Within that logic, planetary degradation, social exploitation at an unprecedented scale, and destruction of cultures make perfect sense if they don't contradict the bottom line. Token measures, largely ineffective, address only the more glaring issues. This is the past that replicates itself, whether it carries the name of capitalism or socialism or any variation thereof.

Yet the future is also present, and hope is present with it. But we need to live within it to detect it. We can no longer look at the past and seek to redeem past ideologies. A consciousness that looks backward demands that we bring this hope to an immediate level of understanding. It is the equivalent of asking for something that can be quickly understood, rather than seeking a patient inner transformation. From that perspective, we cannot understand the future that is already affecting the present.

We have entered the age of networks and the Internet. Social reality is fashioned by ideas that do not have individual origin or ownership, ideas that are in the air, so to speak. Some of the most successful initiatives cannot be traced to a centralized initiative or to a founder, not even to an organization. They emerge when the time is right; they develop organically out of their own inner dynamic. Such was the case for Earth Day. The individuals who carried the impetus knew how to tap into the collective energy that wanted to take a new direction. Julia Butterfly Hill and countless other individuals are doing the same.

Moving into the Future

Well, I've got a hammer and I've got a bell, and I've got a song to sing
all over this land. It's the hammer of justice; It's the bell of freedom; It's a
song about love between my brothers and my sisters, all over this land.
—Pete Seeger and Lee Hays

*T*here is a continuity between the earlier yearnings of the republic
and those that followed and brought us to the twentieth century. It
touches various aspects of the American dream. We review below the
three threads that have formed the leitmotif of the book's exploration.

Toward a New Culture

In speaking of American cultural heroes, we have given center stage to
Washington, Franklin, Lincoln, and Martin Luther King Jr. With each
one of them, the idea of America took a decisive step forward, and the
dream was renewed, even if only for a time.

We have dwelled at length on the figure of Washington. It will
suffice to repeat here that the first president subscribed to the best of
the Freemason ethic, when there was still vitality left in that old ideal.
But that was not the full extent of his personal practice. In him we can
detect something we could call true piety, more than a washed-out
version of Sunday observance. Prayer had a deeply personal meaning
to Washington and was something that sustained him and his mission
in truly difficult times. That devotion was what allowed him to curb his
ambition and impulsiveness and devote them to a larger cause.

Something unique and prophetic of modern times lived in the
old Philadelphia sage, Franklin. With casual nonchalance, Franklin

153

developed a vision of spirituality that lay in accord with science itself. This vision is what he attempted with his exploration of the virtues, with his experiment with vegetarianism, and with his scientific and civic achievements.

Lincoln's strength came from yet another place. It was tempered in the crucible of personal and national ordeals. He had developed a uniquely personal relationship toward anything concerning the essence of the Bible and the Christ figure within it, closest perhaps to what could be described as a very future-oriented Pauline Christianity. It is so puzzling to posterity that it can only be expressed in paradoxes. Historian Nathaniel Stephenson wrote, "His religion continues to resist intellectual formulation." Professor James Randall, the author of four volumes about Lincoln, comments, "Surely, among successful American politicians, Lincoln is unique in the way he breathed the spirit of Christ while disregarding the letter of Christian doctrine."[1]

Martin Luther King Jr. was a preacher as much as an activist. His most famous speech, "I Have a Dream," has been considered a new Gettysburg Address. King originally meant it to be a more sober and factual address. Gary Younge, author of *The Speech*, relates that Clarence Jones, who was present at the event just twenty feet away from King, heard Mahalia Jackson (a close friend of King) shouting more than once, "Tell them about the dream, Martin." Jackson's persistent reminder motivated him to switch from a prosaic platform of grievances to a message that America will never forget.[2] In King, a phenomenal capacity for accurate analysis was present, and it was allied with the courage of spiritual conviction. His insights derived in no small measure from his capacity to transcend dualism, a capacity that he adopted from Hegelian thinking. His gift to the present found full expression in nonviolence and in his capacity to see, or intuit, a third option at a higher level between any two terms of opposition. He tried, in fact, to transcend the capitalism/socialism dualism.

The four individuals listed above, and many others, have reached freedom through the strength of their souls. They reached what we could call the power of one: the power of individuality to change the world around it. We are nearing the time in which the qualities of all these individuals will be found no longer in just one or two leaders, but diffused among many, who are willing to work together and to set themselves goals that are both personal and social, to become the Gandhian "change you want to see in the world."

Reclaiming "We the People"

Our democratic system is based on the central tenet of equality under the law, and the political system has the central task of protecting and expanding this sphere of equality. What was initiated as a new promise for humanity with the American Revolution superseded the failure of the French Revolution. It proved to be so well-conceived that it resisted the trials of time, even though it came out quite battered and weakened in the attempt. Equality is a continuous revelation for generation after generation. Men of the eighteenth century were oblivious to the plight of women, and many were oblivious to the plight of slaves. The issue of equality for these groups came to a head in the following century. No one then would have foreseen the battles for the rights of gay, lesbian, bisexual, and transgender people, nor imagine that the developmentally disabled, too, would claim their share. Can we imagine what will come in the next century?

Significantly, the women's struggle claimed itself to be a continuation of the ideal set forth in the Declaration of Independence. It started in this nation and offered inspiration to many other countries, many of which achieved their goal even before the United States did. At each step of the liberation of African Americans and of women, the constitution expanded. It became more than had been originally conceived, demonstrating that a form of government by and for the people is like a living organism. It is something that grows in parallel with our growing perception and understanding of what it means to be human. In the measure that the constitution can evolve and grow, we receive the guarantee of the vibrancy of our democracy.

Something else has appeared that is essential in the working of democracy and the attainment of true equality, along with the striving for true personal freedom: the capacity of working with what may look like a complete opposite, but is in reality a perfect complement. Over the centuries, the eastern part of the continent has offered us many examples:

Deganawidah and Hiawatha, Franklin and Washington, Elizabeth Cady Stanton and Susan B. Anthony. We may call this the power of two.

The founding of the Haudenosaunee (the Iroquois Confederation) illustrates the working of two very different individuals and was possible only through the work of these differences. Deganawidah had the intuition of what needed to happen. He carried the inspiration of what amounted to a completely new cultural impulse, which set the course of his life. Hiawatha could recognize the validity of the prophet's insights only in the trials and errors of life. But once he seized the message of righteousness, health, and power, he knew how to hold onto it without faltering. In the attempt, he was so thoroughly transformed by it that he could add something new to what Deganawidah had seen; he could embody the message. Hiawatha had gone through the eye of the needle of what it meant to be an Iroquois of the old order, suffering the ills of warfare, cannibalism, and decadent magic. And he had also seen what lay on the other shore before leading the Five Nations.

Franklin and Washington played similar roles to those of their Iroquois counterparts in what was a more dynamic and complex image. They were the two, among many, who embodied two essential personality aspects in the most accomplished way. Franklin held the torch aloft of truly novel ideas for America, France, and the world. Inwardly, he knew what America had to become. Washington became the role model for what this new order would look like if it ever had a chance to become a reality. The first had prepared minds and hearts for decades before the time was ripe. The second carried the ideal in the tumult of the unyielding real world. He steered his course in such a way that the actual could remain close enough to the ideal. He refrained from anything that would have irreversibly compromised the new.

At another level, the integration of polarities was achieved in the women's movement by Elizabeth Cady Stanton, Susan B. Anthony, and Lucy Stone. Here the dynamic was more subtle and differentiated. Cady Stanton formed an ideal temperamental complement to Anthony. The two were balanced out by Lucy Stone. The same was true at the institutional level. The courage, radicalism, and innovative spirit of the NWSA of the first two individuals was balanced out by realism, soberness, and continuity of Lucy's AWSA. NAWSA embodied the full strength of the movement in the integration of its key individuals.

Another thread should not escape notice. It follows American political life through at least some five centuries. The Iroquois were the first to inaugurate the collaboration of equal nations. This was done not only through delicate checks and balances, but also through the art of listening. The ritual of condolence and the restoration of individual harmony were as important as the structure of the Haudenosaunee itself. The Iroquois inaugurated a practice of American social art that has endured through the centuries.

Four centuries after the Iroquois established their confederacy, thus experiencing a turning point in their culture, the union of equals found an echo of its predecessor in the union of the thirteen former colonies. Once again, the art of listening is what made the American experiment a success and the French Revolution a failed experiment. It would be easy to underestimate what patience it took to craft a Declaration of Independence that was agreeable to all or to sit in Philadelphia's summer heat and patiently listen for long hours to all that the delegates had to offer at the Constitutional Convention. Here, too, Franklin and Washington played key roles by ensuring that all participants could be honored and heard and that everyone could examine, with open heart and mind, the new form that emerged. Almost a century later, the women of the East Coast inaugurated years of conventions and other forms of debate. Even the adversaries of the women's movement had to admit to being impressed by the quality and civility of the debates. No doubt the Quaker influence of Lucretia Mott and others played an important part at the beginning.

At present, representative democracy is coming to the end of its rope. The phrase "one dollar, one vote" is the simplest explanation of the present limits. The simple truth is that access to corporate money determines the outcome of a great percentage of legislation. Political parties that divide to conquer, that represent vested economic interests, and that simplify issues to the extreme do not offer much fresh air to a dying democracy.

Surprisingly, however, new ideas and practices are blossoming alongside the dying, which make even direct democracy plausible and effective. We can have a fuller understanding of the whole complexity of issues facing us and tackle them with a much fuller degree of participation than has ever been imagined possible. In other words, complex realities can be apprehended by all stakeholders involved, debated in common, and deliberated in such a way that solutions emerge that satisfy all parties involved to a degree that our representative democracy has long ceased to do.

We are no longer looking at the integration of the contribution of diverse individuals, but at the integration, rather, of whole sectors of society, and the acceptance that we need to incorporate what seem like polar opposite sectors of society. This requires the willingness to transform one's own perceptions and ideas before attempting to change society. We have all witnessed the fresh air brought by the Occupy Wall Street movement. What stood out for this author (and for many people I know) was, once again, the civility of the consensus process of the OWS general assembly and the ability to include all voices in what many feared would be nothing else than a cacophony. And yet, the OWS general assemblies could really discern the will of the whole.

The Call for Economic Justice

Finally, the quest for economic justice, for a world in which we attend to each other's needs like brothers and sisters, evolved since the birth of the nation. It first looked inward, then outward. It found expression in two American holidays: Thanksgiving and Earth Day. Thanksgiving looks inward to what Martin Luther King Jr. called "the beloved community," which in America expresses a microcosm of the world, bringing together a maximum of diversity of expression, whether racially, culturally, or religiously. This force expressed itself at first as America's reaction against British imperialism, which rendered all such concepts clearly impossible. Thanksgiving is a first worldwide recognition, in the form of a holiday, of the brotherhood of the human race. A nation recognized that all its citizens are equal because in them the divine is equally expressed.

Thanksgiving lost much of its original significance as time passed. Earth Day renewed and expanded this American longing and allowed us at the same time to look outward. America, now having become the center of world empire, is the cause of much of the global upheaval that manifests in the economic and ecological crisis, and now in climate change. This painful recognition of the evils of empire became for some the rallying cry for a global consciousness, united with a growing awareness of the earth as a living being. Earth Day signaled at the same time a new awareness of the world predicament and of the interconnectedness of all human beings, a "world Thanksgiving," of sorts. Over and against the growing reality of empire, the American soul recognizes the need for another type of economic growth, one that respects world cultures, sovereign nations, equitable social relationships, and the environment. More and more movements are realizing the relationships between the negative effects within all the areas listed above and their root causes in world economy run amuck. The realization is growing that there will be no fair share of the fruits of the global economy under the present free-market system.

We no longer live closed off in a national identity, shielded from the world at large. We are realizing that we are part of an extended tapestry of destiny, as Martin Luther King Jr. would have expressed it. And all issues are related to, and derived from, a world economy that has usurped the political arena and the role of culture. The landmark US Supreme Court acceptance of corporations as individuals fittingly illustrates the usurpation of culture by corporations such as Coke, Microsoft, and McDonald's. Under the economic reality of globalization, with the consequent destruction of cultures worldwide, it behooves all American idealists to trace the links between one issue and the other.

It is globalization, as it is presently conceived, that generates one ecological crisis after the other, and at present, climate change. It is the present economic model that consumes our planet faster than it can regenerate. It is this economy that renders human beings dispensable and robs them of meaningful work and of an expression of their being in the world. It is this world economy that squeezes people like lemons in thousands of sweatshops from Mexico to Bangladesh, to China and throughout the third world. It is this economy that is creating growing economic disparity and poverty within the most powerful nation in the world, a nation that once was described as a beacon and example for the globe. It is within this country that citizens are now affected even in the most vital matters of health. The country's wealth is no longer a guarantee that its citizens can have access to health; far from it. And the dictates of the economy no longer have room for what used to be thought of as the commons, nor for individual privacy or freedom. America is hardly the land of opportunity, nor the dream it could be.

The response to this global challenge lies in the power of networks. We are witnessing in America and worldwide what change is possible through self-organization of myriads of movements. Julia Butterfly Hill's activism, sitting in a giant Sequoia tree for two years, brought together two important factors for social change: labor and environmentalism. The Earth Day coalition did the same at the national and international levels. Myriads of organizations converged. The 1999 "Battle of Seattle" brought together many organizations and created vast networks. Beyond resisting the trends of the past, people in the United States are also actively promoting economic models for the future. Organic agriculture is spreading its stewardship of the land, and community-supported agriculture is forming a complete new model for consumer-producer relationships. The network for fair trade is doing this at an international level. Seeds of new economic models are present in the ideas of land trusts, cohousing, and eco-villages, where the ownership moves, to various degrees, from the individual to larger collective entities. Thousands of investors now turn to socially responsible investing, one of the most reliable forms of investment.

America can again be the land of the free, it can be the land where all human beings are equal, and it can be the land of opportunity. Our culture can be strengthened to the point that we know what it is to be truly free, creative, mature individuals like Franklin, Washington, Lincoln, and King. We can enlarge our political system in such a way that all voices are heard and every citizen is truly equal. Finally, although it may take the longest of all these changes, we can take part in renewing the economy so that we are truly stewards of the earth and of each other. We stand at the threshold of either the globalization of a higher consciousness or the globalization of denial. Truly courageous choices in radial departure from the past can allow a future for a truly compassionate America, a home to freedom, equality, and social justice.

Notes and References

Chapter 1

1) Samuel L. Mitchill, *The Life, Exploits and Precepts of Tammany, the Famous Indian Chief.*

2) Charles C. Conley, George W. Lindsay, and Charles H. Litchman, *Official History of the Improved Order of Red Men*, 158–159.

3) The Pennsylvania Magazine of History and Biography, Vol. XXVI, No. 29, pp. 443-463.

4) Edwin P. Kilroe, *Saint Tammany and the Origin of the Society of Tammany or Columbian Order in the City of New York*, 32, 38–39, 94.

5) Mitchill, *The Life, Exploits and Precepts of Tammany.*

6) Charles C. Conley, George W. Lindsay, and Charles H. Litchman, *Official History of the Improved Order of Red Men*; see chapter 4: Society of Red Men (1813–1833). From this document we have insight into the importance of ritual and the blending of typical Masonic ceremonies with Native American overtones. The applicants had to be proposed by a brother. A committee would then inquire into the candidate's fitness and character. Acceptance had to be subscribed by a unanimous vote. Later, the neophyte would be placed under the tutelage of the doorkeeper, who offered him instruction and presented him to the generalissimo. The would-be member was questioned regarding his citizenship and his motives for seeking to join, and was warned that "Red Men are men without fear, and that none but such could be grafted into the tribe."

    Once again the neophyte would be presented to the generalissimo for further instructions. Part of these read: "Red Men administer no oaths binding you to any political or religious creed.... The motto of the society is 'freedom,' and while claiming its privileges and blessings for ourselves, we aim no less to exert toleration to others." This was followed by a request for trustworthiness and faithfulness to their ideals. Additionally the neophyte had to keep the rituals secret from the uninitiated. After adoption, the society conferred on the new member a hierarchical title and a new name in the Indian tradition. In secret ceremonies, only Native American names were used.

7) Kilroe, *Saint Tammany and the Origin of the Society of Tammany*, 42.

8) Douglas Southall Freeman, *Washington: An Abridgment of the 7-Volume Opus*, 154.

9) The following are some examples of the measures taken by the Trade Board:

1699: prohibition of exportation of wool, yarn, and woolen cloth from one colony to the other

1705: Pennsylvania law encouraging shoemaking industry disallowed by the Board

1706–08 rejection of Virginia and Maryland laws to provide for the establishment of new towns

1732: prohibition of export of hats

1750: prohibition of the erection of slitting or rolling mills and of plate, forge, or steel furnaces

1756: nullification of Massachusetts ordinance encouraging the production of linen

10) Murray N. Rothbard, *Conceived in Liberty*, 212–213.

11) In *Patriarch: George Washington and the New American Nation*, Richard Norton Smith has documented the nature of the exchanges between Hamilton and George Hammond, British envoy to the United States, and how these undermined the diplomatic efforts between the two countries.

12) In this regard see: Conor Cruise O'Brien, *The Long Affair: Thomas Jefferson and the French Revolution: 1785–1800*. Although Thomas Jefferson's passion for violent revolution was only one phase in his life, it preceded the French Revolution itself and continued into the years he spent in France. In relation to the Shays' Rebellion of 1776, Jefferson wrote, "God forbid we should be twenty years without such a rebellion. The people cannot be all, and always, well informed … Let them take arms. The remedy is to set them right as to facts, pardon and pacify them. What signify a few lives lost in a century or two. The tree of liberty must be refreshed from time to time with the blood of patriots and tyrants. It is its natural manure" (letter to William Stephen Smith of November 13, 1787, in *The Long Affair*, pp. 41–42).

Jefferson's revolutionary enthusiasm was strengthened by the French Revolution. In a letter to William Short, Jefferson urges the diplomat not to complain about the excesses of the French Revolution, but to accept that there is no limit to the slaughter that is allowed in the cause of freedom. Here is one quote: "The liberty of the whole earth was depending on the issue of the contest, and was ever such a prize won with so little innocent blood? My own affections have been deeply wounded by some of the martyrs to this cause, but rather than it should have failed, I would have seen half the earth desolated. Were there but an Adam & an Eve left in every country, & left free, it would be better than as it now is" (the "Adam and Eve" letter from Thomas Jefferson to William Short, January 3, 1793, pp. 145–147). In personal notes on a conversation with George Washington, Jefferson remembers that his support for the French Revolution had been his "polar star" and records that Washington supposedly was a late convert to the cause (from Conor Cruise O'Brien, *The Long Affair: Thomas Jefferson and the French Revolution, 1785–1800*).

13) Susan B. Martinez, *The Psychic Life of Abraham Lincoln*, 87-89, quoting the *National Tribune*, December 1880 (vol. 4, no. 12).

14) Patricia U. Bonomi, *Under the Cope of Heaven: Religion, Society, and Politics in Colonial America*, 195.

Chapter 2

1) Nancy Bonvillain, *Hiawatha: Founder of the Iroquois Confederacy.* 11-51.

2) Ibid, 23.

3) Horatio Hale, *The Iroquois Book of Rites*, 31.

4) Bruce E. Johansen, *Forgotten Founders: How the American Indians Helped Shape Democracy.*

5) In 1688 England, wanting to avoid the risk of a return to Catholicism through James II, offered the crown to James's anti-Catholic daughter and her husband, William, Prince of Orange. The house of Orange (house of Hanover) had been Britain's archenemy a century before. The move left many wounds in the country. Although Scotland became part of England in 1689 without bloodshed, the Scots remained loyal to the House of Stuart, as did most of Freemasonry. The birth in 1717 of the Grand Lodge was for all intents the attempt of the Hanoverian house to break the exclusive Stuart influence on Freemasonry.

6) Esmond Wright, *Franklin of Philadelphia*, 354.

7) Carl Van Doren, *Benjamin Franklin*, 143–146.

8) Esmond Wright, ed., *Benjamin Franklin: His Life as He Wrote It*, 102.

9) Johansen, *Forgotten Founders: How the American Indians Helped Shape Democracy*, 56.

10) Ibid, 61–62.

11) Nelson Beecher Keyes, *Ben Franklin: An Affectionate Portrait*, 239.

12) Baigent and Leigh, *The Temple and the Lodge*, 255.

13) Ibid, 217.

14) Ibid, 214.

Chapter 3

1) Joyce K. Kessel and Lisa Donze, *Squanto and the First Thanksgiving*; Clyde Robert Bulla, *Squanto, Friend of the Pilgrims*.

2) Murray Rothbard, "The Virginia Company," *Conceived in Liberty*, vol. 1.

3) Frances Mossiker, *Pocahontas: The Life and the Legend*, 273.

4) Philip L. Barbour, *The Three Worlds of Captain John Smith*, 308; Leo Bonfanti, *Biographies and Legends of the New England Indians*, vol. 2, 22.

5) Barbour, *The Three Worlds of Captain John Smith*, 314.

6) Ibid, 343–344.

7) Ibid, 341–347.

8) Most information concerning Squanto is taken from Bonfanti, *Biographies and Legends of the New England Indians*. Additional information is taken from Feenie Ziner, *Squanto*.

9) Ziner, *Squanto*, notes to p. 146.

10) Most of the information concerning Pocahontas is taken from Mossiker, *Pocahontas: The Life and the Legend*.

11) It is with Reverend Whitaker that Pocahontas had the most untarnished meeting of minds. Whitaker was a Puritan and a scholar, son of a master and regius professor of divinity. He had been destined to a successful career in England; his renunciation of a life of comfort and recognition indicates the depth of his vocation. It is Whitaker who encouraged Rolfe to overcome his hesitations and take the step of marrying the barbarian princess. Whitaker was touched by the depth of Pocahontas's acceptance of Christianity. Whether for that reason or others, he recognized of the Indians that "They have reasonable soules and intellectuall faculties as well as wee; we all have Adam for our common parent; yea, by nature the condition of us both is all one" (Mossiker, *Pocahontas: The Life and the Legend*, 165).

Chapter 4

1) Diana Karter Appelbaum, *Thanksgiving: An American Holiday, an American History.*

2) Paul Calore, *The Causes of the Civil War: The Political, Cultural, Economic and Territorial Disputes between North and South*, 6.

3) Ibid, 7.

4) James Lardner and David A. Smith, eds., *Inequality Matters: The Growing Economic Divide in America and Its Poisonous Consequences. State of Working America 2004/2005*, tables 1.12 and 4.3.

Chapter 5

1) Stephen B. Oates, *Builders of the Dream: Abraham Lincoln and Martin Luther King Jr.*, 15.

2) Stephen B. Oates, *Let the Trumpet Sound: A Life of Martin Luther King.*

3) Ibid, 47.

4) Christmas 1957 sermon, delivered at the Montgomery Dexter Avenue Baptist Church). See full speech at: http://www.salsa.net/peace/conv/8weekconv4-2.html

5) Oates, *Let the Trumpet Sound*, 372.

6) Ibid, 369.

7) Ibid, 283

8) Ibid, 283.

9) Ibid, 89.

10) Ibid, 110.

11) Ibid, 111.

12) Ibid, 466.

13) Ibid, 484.

14) Ibid, 485.

15) Adam Fairclough, (1983). "Was Martin Luther King a Marxist?" 117-125.

16) Speech delivered at New York City's Riverside Church on April 4, 1967. See: http://www.spiritofmaat.com/messages/oct7/mlk.htm

17) Oates, *Let the Trumpet Sound*, 101.

18) See full speech at: http://mlk-kpp01.stanford.edu/index.php/ encyclopedia/documentsentry/doc give us the ballot address at the prayer pilgrimage for freedom/

19) Oates, *Let the Trumpet Sound*, 223.

20) Ibid, 452.

21) Martin Luther King Jr., *Where Do We Go from Here: Chaos or Community?* 181–182.

22) Ibid., 197.

Chapter 6

1) Jean H. Baker, *Sisters: The Lives of America's Suffragists*, 10.

2) Sally Roesch Wagner, *Sisters in Spirit: Haudenosaunee (Iroquois) Influence on Early American Feminists*, 32, 44.

3) Ibid, 42.

4) Sally G. McMillen, *Seneca Falls and the Origins of the Women's Rights Movement*, 109.

5) Ibid, 87.

6) Ibid, 87.

7) Baker, *Sisters: The Lives of America's Suffragists*, 87.

8) Ibid, 89.

9) Ibid, 91

10) McMillen, *Seneca Falls and the Origins of the Women's Rights Movement*, 155.

11) Baker, *Sisters: The Lives of America's Suffragists*, 161.

12) Ibid, 200.

13) Ibid, 199.

14) McMillen, *Seneca Falls and the Origins of the Women's Rights Movement*, 242-250.

15) Baker, *Sisters: The Lives of America's Suffragists*, 221.

Chapter 7

1) http://en.wikipedia.org/wiki/John_McConnell_(peace_activist).

2) http://en.wikipedia.org/wiki/Gaylord_Nelson.

3) http://en.wikipedia.org/wiki/Denis_Hayes.

4) http://en.wikipedia.org/wiki/Pete_McCloskey.

5) Julia Butterfly Hill, *The Legacy of Luna: The Story of a Tree, a Woman, and the Struggle to Save the Redwoods.*

6) Ibid, 5.

7) Ibid, 8.

8) Ibid,11.

9) Ibid, 121-122.

10) Ibid, 66.

11) Ibid, 107.

12) Ibid, 113.

13) Ibid, 114.

14) Ibid, 115.

15) Ibid, 130.

16) Ibid, 171

17) Ibid, 198.

Conclusions

1) William J. Wolf, *Lincoln's Religion*, 192.

2) From an interview of Gary Younge with Amy Goodman. See: *http://www.democracynow.org/2013/8/21/50 years later the untold history*

Bibliography

Applebaum, Diana Karter. *Thanksgiving: An American Holiday, an American History*. New York: Facts on File Publications, 1984.

Baker, Jean H. *Sisters: The Lives of America's Suffragists*. New York: Hill and Wang, 2005.

Baigent and Leigh, The Temple and the Lodge. New York : Arcade Publishing, 1989.

Beecher Keyes, Nelson, *Ben Franklin: An Affectionate Portrait*. Garden City, N.Y.: Hanover House, 1956.

Barbour, Philip L. *The Three Worlds of Captain John Smith*. Boston: Houghton Mifflin Company, 1964.

Bonfanti, Leo. *Biographies and Legends of the New England Indians*, vol. 2. Burlington MA: Pride Publications, 1993.

Bonomi, Patricia U. *Under the Cope of Heaven: Religion, Society, and Politics in Colonial America*. Oxford: Oxford University Press, 1986.

Bonvillain, Nancy. *Hiawatha: Founder of the Iroquois Confederacy*. New York: Chelsea House Publishers, 1992.

Bulla, Clyde Robert. *Squanto, Friend of the Pilgrims*. New York: Scholastic Inc., 1954.

Calore, Paul. *The Causes of the Civil War: The Political, Cultural, Economic and Territorial Disputes between North and South*. Jefferson, NC: McFarland and Company Inc., 2008.

Conley, Charles C., George W. Lindsay, and Charles H. Litchman. *Official History of the Improved Order of Red Men.* Boston: The Fraternity Publishing Co., 1893.

Fairclough, Adam "Was Martin Luther King a Marxist?" History Workshop Journal 1983, 15 (1), http://hwj.oxfordjournals.org/cgi/pdf_extract/15/1/117

Freeman, Douglas Southall. *Washington,* abridgement by Richard Harwell. New York: Charles Scribners' Sons, 1985.

Hale, Horatio. *The Iroquois Book of Rites.* New York: AMS Press, 1969.

Hill, Julia Butterfly. *The Legacy of Luna: The Story of a Tree, a Woman, and the Struggle to Save the Redwoods.* San Francisco, CA: Harper San Francisco, 2000.

Johansen, Bruce E. *Forgotten Founders: How the American Indians Helped Shape Democracy.* Boston: The Harvard Common Press, 1982.

Kessel, Joyce K., and Lisa Donze. *Squanto and the First Thanksgiving.* Minneapolis: Carolrhoda Books, 1983.

Keyes, Nelson Beecher. *Ben Franklin: An Affectionate Portrait.* Garden City, NY: Hanover House, 1956.

Kilroe, Edwin P. *Saint Tammany and the Origin of the Society of Tammany or Columbian Order in the City of New York.* New York: M. B. Brown, 1913.

King, Martin Luther Jr. *Where Do We Go from Here: Chaos or Community?* Boston: Beacon Press, 1967.

Lardner, James and Smith, David A. eds., *Inequality Matters: The Growing Economic Divide in America and Its Poisonous Consequences. State of Working America 2004/2005*New York: The New Press, 2005.

Martinez, Susan B. *The Psychic Life of Abraham Lincoln.* Franklin Lakes, NJ: Career Press, 2009.

McMillen, Sally G. *Seneca Falls and the Origins of the Women's Rights Movement*. New York: Oxford University Press, 2008.

Mitchill, Samuel Latham. *The Life, Exploits and Precepts of Tammany, the Famous Indian Chief*. Oration delivered at Old Presbyterian Church, New York, on May 12, 1795, microfilm.

Mossiker, Frances. *Pocahontas: The Life and the Legend*. New York: Da Capo Press, 1996.

Oates, Stephen B. *Builders of the Dream: Abraham Lincoln and Martin Luther King Jr.* Fort Wayne, IN: Louis A. Warren Lincoln Library and Museum, 1982.

Oates, Stephen B. *Let the Trumpet Sound: A Life of Martin Luther King.* New York: Harper Collins Publishers, 1982.

O'Brien, Conor C. *The Long Affair: Thomas Jefferson and the French Revolution: 1785–1800.* Chicago: University of Chicago Press, 1998.

Parker, Arthur C. *Parker on the Iroquois.* Syracuse, NY: Syracuse University Press, 1968.

Roesch Wagner, Sally. *Sisters in Spirit: Haudenosaunee (Iroquois) Influence on Early American Feminists.* Summertown, TN: Book Publishing Company, 2001.

Rothbard, Murray N. *Conceived in Liberty.* (New Rochelle, NY: Arlington House Publishers, 1975.

Smith, Richard Norton. *Patriarch: George Washington and the New American Nation.* Boston & New York: Houghton Mifflin, 1993.

Van Doren, Carl. *Benjamin Franklin.* New York: Penguin Books, 1938.

Wolf, William J. *Lincoln's Religion*, 1970 ed. Philadelphia & Boston: Pilgrim Press, 1959.

Wright, Esmond. *Franklin of Philadelphia*. Cambridge, MA: Belknap Press, Harvard University Press, 1986.

_____, ed. *Benjamin Franklin: His Life as He Wrote It*. Cambridge, MA: Harvard University Press, 1989.

Younge, Gary. *The Speech: The Story behind Dr. Martin Luther King Jr.'s Dream*. Chicago: Haymarket Books, 2013.

Ziner, Feenie. *Squanto*. Hamden, CN: Linnet Books, 1988.

Internet Sources

Democracy Now
http://www.democracynow.
org/2013/8/21/50_years_later_the_untold_history

Salsa.net
http://www.salsa.net/peace/conv/8weekconv4-2.html

Spirit of Maat
http://www.spiritofmaat.com/messages/oct7/mlk.htm

Stanford.edu
http://mlk-kpp01.stanford.edu/index.php/encyclopedia/documentsentry/doc_give_us_the_ballot_address_at_the_prayer_pilgrimage_for_freedom/

Wikipedia
http://en.wikipedia.org/wiki/John_McConnell_(peace_activist).

http://en.wikipedia.org/wiki/Gaylord_Nelson.

http://en.wikipedia.org/wiki/Denis_Hayes.

http://en.wikipedia.org/wiki/Pete_McCloskey

Open Book Editions
A Berrett-Koehler Partner

Open Book Editions is a joint venture between Berrett-Koehler Publishers and Author Solutions, the market leader in self-publishing. There are many more aspiring authors who share Berrett-Koehler's mission than we can sustainably publish. To serve these authors, Open Book Editions offers a comprehensive self-publishing opportunity.

A Shared Mission

Open Book Editions welcomes authors who share the Berrett-Koehler mission—Creating a World That Works for All. We believe that to truly create a better world, action is needed at all levels—individual, organizational, and societal. At the individual level, our publications help people align their lives with their values and with their aspirations for a better world. At the organizational level, we promote progressive leadership and management practices, socially responsible approaches to business, and humane and effective organizations. At the societal level, we publish content that advances social and economic justice, shared prosperity, sustainability, and new solutions to national and global issues.

Open Book Editions represents a new way to further the BK mission and expand our community. We look forward to helping more authors challenge conventional thinking, introduce new ideas, and foster positive change.

For more information, see the Open Book Editions website:
http://www.iuniverse.com/Packages/OpenBookEditions.aspx

Join the BK Community! See exclusive author videos, join discussion groups, find out about upcoming events, read author blogs, and much more! http://bkcommunity.com/